CIRCUIT RIDERS ON THE ROAD TO GLORY

D. Gregory Van Dussen

*The Asbury Theological Seminary Series in World Christian
Revitalization Movements in Pietist/Wesleyan Studies*

EMETH PRESS
www.emethpress.com

Circuit Riders on the Road to Glory

Copyright © 2020 D. Gregory Van Dussen
Printed in the United States of America on acid-free paper

All rights reserved. No part of this book may be reproduced, or stored in a retrieval system or transmitted in any form or by any means, lectronic, mechanical, photocopying, recording, scanning or otherwise, except as permitted by the 1976 United States Copyright Act, or with the prior written permission of Emeth Press. Requests for permission should be addressed to: Emeth Press, 7216 S. Ridgetop Ct., Dardenne Prairie, MO 63368 http://www.emethpress.com.

Library of Congress Cataloging-in-Publication Data

Names: Van Dussen, D. Gregory, author.
Title: Circuit riders on the road to glory / D. Gregory Van Dussen.
Description: Dardenne Prairie, MO : Emeth Press, [2020] | Series: Asbury Theological Seminary series in Pietist/Wesleyan studies | Summary: "This book guides readers on a journey into the history of the early Methodist faith as preached and believed by those who embraced the very difficult and demanding lifestyle of the circuit-riding preacher. Covering hundreds of miles on horseback and sometimes by foot, these early ministers traveled the wilderness to spread the gospel"-- Provided by publisher.
Identifiers: LCCN 2020048537 (print) | LCCN 2020048538 (ebook) | ISBN 9781609471668 (paperback : acid-free paper) | ISBN 9781609471675 (kindle edition)
Subjects: LCSH: Methodist Church--United States--History. | Circuit riders--United States--History.
Classification: LCC BX8235 .V36 2020 (print) | LCC BX8235 (ebook) | DDC 287.092/273--dc23
LC record available at https://lccn.loc.gov/2020048537
LC ebook record available at https://lccn.loc.gov/2020048538

Endorsements for Circuit Riders on the Road to Glory

Van Dussen provides a thoughtful survey of Circuit Rider ministry in an enjoyable and accessible text. He brings to life a host of important voices and paints an honest picture of the motivations and struggles behind this harrowing call. While being true to the historical figures, Van Dussen carefully weaves a thread of important messages for contemporary Christians. Readers will find this book well worth their time as they encounter remarkable examples of lives framed around hope in Christ. Traveling with this company on the "Road to Glory" provides powerful inspiration for Christians and an invitation to shift our perspectives toward the eternal.
 —Rev. Dr. J.L. Miller, Associate Dean of the Chapel, Houghton College

Methodist circuit riders played a significant role in shaping North American Christianity. Van Dussen takes us beyond the stories of their meanderings and methods to reveal their message – a deep passion to pursue John Wesley's "way to heaven." Using primary texts from 19th century preachers and biographers, he reveals a North American interpretation of Wesleyan theology and shows how it might be applied in our present context. Here you can read their own words of passion and hope for an eternal destiny. Voices from the past call us to the same commitment to save souls and send them down the glory road to a richer life and an eternal kingdom.
 —Dr. Bud Bence, Emeritus Professor of Church History, Indiana Wesleyan University

Contents

Foreword / v

Introduction / ix

Chapter 1. Motivation / 1

Chapter 2. Beginnings / 9

Chapter 3. Expectation / 19

Chapter 4. Invitation / 25

Chapter 5. Distraction / 31

Chapter 6. Vision / 43

Chapter 7. Perspective / 55

Chapter 8. Companions / 63

Chapter 9. Resources / 69

Chapter 10. Transformation / 81

Chapter 11. Worship / 89

Chapter 12. Transition / 101

Chapter 13. Direction / 117

Chapter 14. Peculiarities / 125

Chapter 15. Application / 135

Dedication

Circuit Riders on the Road to Glory is dedicated to the people with whom I have walked this road, especially those I have served as youth pastor, pastor, retired pastor, or district superintendent.

West Avenue United Methodist Church, Rochester, NY
Batavia First UM Church, Batavia, NY
Cattaraugus UM Church, Cattaraugus, NY
Wesley UM Church, Gowanda, NY
Bergen UM Church, Bergen, NY
First UM Church, Albion, NY
Batavia District, Batavia, NY
Baker Memorial UM Church, East Aurora, NY
Springville First UM Church, Springville, NY
Indian Falls UM Church, Corfu, NY

Foreword

During the late eighteenth and early nineteenth centuries, a religious revival swept across North America. Emphasizing the redemption of sins through faith rather than good works, enthusiastic traveling preachers defined the Christian life as a journey that leads to heaven. In the small isolated communities and far flung territories of the United States and Canada, people by the hundreds gathered to hear this message of hope.

In Circuit Riders on the Road to Glory, Dr. Greg Van Dussen, pastor and historian, guides readers on a journey into the history of the early Wesleyan faith as preached and believed by those who embraced the very difficult and demanding lifestyle of the circuit-riding preacher. Covering hundreds of miles on horseback and sometimes by foot, these early ministers traveled the wilderness to spread the gospel of transformation brought about by a one-on-one relationship with God through His Son Jesus Christ. They believed that the Christian's earthly journey engenders spiritual growth and that heartfelt worship offers a foretaste of the indescribable joy believers will experience in heaven.

A familiar verse in the Old Testament book of Micah well describes the circuit rider's mindset. "And what does the Lord require of you? To act justly and to love mercy and to walk humbly with your God." (Micah 6:8b NIV)

Disavowing the prejudices common at the time, these ministers reached out to free and slave alike, to women as well as men, to Native American peoples, and also to the most down-trodden and underprivileged populations in North America. During this renewal, the African Methodist Episcopal Church and the African Methodist Episcopal Zion Church were founded, and, through the circuit-riders' ministry, the anti-slavery movement found new strength. Women formed prayer groups, and thus their influence spread beyond the home into the wider community, paving the way for the long fight that would eventually establish a woman's right to vote. Through the circuit riders' ministry, people experienced the transforming power of God. Families were reunited, the broken were healed, and love and hope inspired lives of dedication and caring.

As a history of miracles and hardships, Dr. Van Dussen's Circuit Riders on the Road to Glory assures Christians of today that "I can do all this through him who gives me strength." (Philippians 4:13 NIV).

> Sue Harrison
> Author of
> The Ivory Carver Trilogy
> The Storyteller Trilogy

"...we see the *eternal world*, piercing through the veil which hangs between time and eternity. Clouds and darkness then rest upon it no more, but we already see the glory which shall be revealed."

> John Wesley, "*The Scripture Way of Salvation,*" in Kenneth J. Collins and Jason E. Vickers, eds. *The Sermon of John Wesley: A Collection for the ChristianJourney.* Nashville, Abingdon, 2013, 585.

"The essence of service ... is the transmission of eternal life to the children whom God has placed in our charge."

> Matthew the Poor, *If You Love Me: Serving Christ and the Church in Spirit and Truth.* Chesterton, IN: Ancient Faith, 1971, 29.

Introduction

"Blessed are those whose strength is in you, whose hearts are set on pilgrimage." —*Psalms 84:5, NIV*

"Born that man no more may die...." Charles Wesley, "Hark! The Herald Angels Sing," *Hymns of Faith and Life,* Winona Lake, IN: *Light and Life,* Marion, IN: Wesley Press, 1976 #117, v. 3.

What is traveling like for you? Preparations may not be your favorite part, but they're vital to any trip's success. The road to your destination can be wonderful, stressful, challenging, or all three. Who will guide you on your journey? Who will travel with you? What is your destination, the reason you're setting out on this venture in the first place? What resources will you need to make this journey? How will you access food and drink along the way? Where will you stop when your fuel is running low? What will keep you going when the going gets rough?

Christian life is a journey, one that asks all these questions and more. It does not meander aimlessly or without purpose. Our clear goal is the kingdom of heaven, which we experience in part while we're still on the journey. (John 3:36) Our guide is the One who called us to this journey, Jesus Christ. We share this journey with everyone who responds to that call and follows his leadership. He provides us with everything we need to make a success out of this journey, in good times and bad. While we're on the way to heaven, he works through us to bring heaven to those around us.

An old folk song says "This train is bound for glory." Where are *you* bound? If God's glorious kingdom is your destination, and Jesus is your guide, you and your companions have chosen the right road.

Early Methodists embarked on that journey, which the Bible calls "the path of life," —*Psalms 16:11, NIV*; Daniel Wise, *The Path of Life: Or, Sketches of the Way to Glory and Immortality, a Help for Young Christians.* New York: Carlton & Porter, 1847. There were other journeys and other paths available, each with its own promises and requirements, but none could equal the one they chose. Some paths are dead ends. Some guides will mislead you, promising more than they can deliver. Some destinations are not worth your time. But the road to glory is worth everything. On the Christian journey, your path, guide, and goal can all be trusted. Since there is "no permanent home on earth," each one of us "is emphatically a pilgrim and a stranger." —Sermon in Erwin House, *The Homilist.* New York: Carlton & Porter, 1860, 190.

Circuit riding preachers in the Wesleyan tradition chose not only to walk this path, but to continually invite others to join them on the journey. Nathan Bangs made this clear when he described his mission to a Canadian audience in 1801: "I am bound for the heavenly city, and my errand among you is to persuade as many as I can to go with me." —Abel Stevens, *Life and Times of Nathan Bangs, D.D.* New York: Carlton & Porter, 1863, 137.

Their road to glory involved a distinctive way of life, rooted in God's purpose and destiny for humanity and creation itself. That way of life was spiritual, ethical, and even organizational. Individual believers were part of a disciplined community, walking the road together, encouraging each other along the way, bringing people back when they wandered off the path. Their road was one of progressive change toward the full recovery of God's image in each person, always empowered by grace. The destination was "the heavenly city," eternal, infinite life in God's kingdom. —See Adam Clarke. *Christian Theology,* Salem, OH: H.E. Schmul, 1967, 376-380. Everything they said and did was designed to move them closer to that destination, yet their lives and ministries also changed the world around them, for the world itself shares in God's purpose. The journey was one of comprehensive discipleship that left no area of life untouched. Everything was gathered up in a vision of God's new creation, and each one knew he or she had a vital part in bringing that vision about. In that hopeful, activist era, their movement swept across the continent with amazing power and speed.

Comprehensive discipleship flowed from sanctifying grace, the power that transformed hearts, minds, and actions to reflect the character and purpose of God. One's heart came increasingly to reflect God's love. One's thinking was renewed so that it conformed to the "the mind of Christ," the One who is the truth. (Romans 12:2; I Corinthians 2:16; John 14:6). While teaching, writing, and study were extremely important, this was not what James K.A. Smith calls "sanctification by information transfer." As Smith reminds us, "It's not only our minds that God redeems, but the whole person: head, heart, hands." —James K.A. Smith, *You Are What You Love.* Grand Rapids: Brazos, 2016, 4&9. The trajectory of one's life must align with God's ultimate purpose. All of this made up the fabric of "Scripture-holiness" and its march "over these lands" was accomplished in connexion with others who poured themselves into its realization. —*The Doctrines and Discipline of the Methodist Episcopal Church.* Philadelphia: Henry Tuckniss, 1797, iii. The same movement that changed individual lives also built colleges and energized manifold reform movements in American and Canadian society.

The quest for Christian perfection was much more than a positive disposition, correct doctrine, or enforced adherence to a set of rules. Nothing less than a transfigured person in a transfigured community would fulfill their God-given purpose. None of it was accomplished by human will, fortitude, or persistence, though each person needed to cooperate voluntarily, energetically and synergistically with transforming grace, moving forward according to God's desire for humanity and all creation. This was infinitely more than mere altruism or its political expressions.

These early preachers and those they served knew themselves called by God to their tasks. God worked through their distinctive personalities and circumstances so that the movement they led was a vast, multifaceted whole. They were people of their time, yet their mission was timeless. That mission reached back to the New Testament (and beyond), forward to our own time, and onward "to the very end of the age." (Matthew 28:20, NIV) Their movement was filled with excitement and adventure, involving considerable self-sacrifice, yet it shared, lamentably, in our human propensity for selfishness, conflict, confusion, failure, and even rebellion. Like participants in any journey, they could lose their way amid distractions, temporal concerns, and limited wisdom. They could be blown off course by the winds of culture. Yet their vision and accomplishments stand as a powerful witness to the transforming presence of God in this world, and the undying hope of the gospel. In our own time of selfishness, conflict, confusion, failure, and even rebellion, that witness can reawaken us to God's presence and open us to his limitless power.

The central importance of the way of salvation is clear from the continual Methodist struggle against Calvinism. In this debate, Calvinists and Methodists both focused on the eternal destiny of believers, though in radically different ways. —See R.S. Foster, *Objections to Calvinism.* Cincinnati: Methodist Book Concern, 1850. Their differences generated such animated preaching and apologetic writing because so much was at stake. Had life after death been a minor part of their theologies, they might not have expended so much energy, but in fact, the Gospel itself loses ultimate significance without a vision of eternity. "The path of life" – what John Wesley called the way to heaven – *goes somewhere.* (Psalm 16:11, NIV) Its design is for more than improving life for its immediate participants. God is leading us through this life in a way that transforms us for this life *and beyond*. Methodism saw life whole, not in cross-section. The grave was and is a milestone on a much longer journey.

Time and time again these early preachers would reaffirm their Biblical, Wesleyan vision. Most of all, they would return without fail to the Source of that vision, as the power and glory of the Holy Spirit descended upon church, campground, or wilderness solitude. Worship renewed their connection with God. It was their reliable conduit of grace. In worship they lifted their hearts in praise, cried out for mercy, and sang and shouted their thanksgiving. Worship provided strength for the journey, through mutual encouragement and the renewing, transforming power of God in their midst. When it came time to leave this world and enter the next, they would often testify to a sense of peace and fulfillment, trust and visible glory. Prayer and worship accompanied their transition to the destiny they had been seeking all along. Although the Wesleyan family in North America divided often, sometimes for tragically serious reasons, all trace their heritage to common origins in the ministry of John and Charles Wesley and the beginnings of our movement in North America. While the movement was always larger than a single organization, all shared a common purpose, though they sometimes differed as to how best to carry it out. The deepest and most destructive division concerned slavery and failure to maintain the enduring mandate of Methodism's anti-slavery origins. The damage and pain inherent in that division remain with us today. Other issues, especially the shape and exercise of authority, also produced difficult separations. Conflict among denominations and exaggerated moral strictures obscured common Christian values. Yet there was always common ground – beliefs, practices, and experiences shared by the entire fragmented family, especially in the period between its North American beginnings and the Civil War.

Today, Methodists of every grouping have much to gain from a renewal in awareness of their tradition, and, most of all, in the purpose that brought their movement into being. We have much to learn from each other, rich experiences of fellowship and ministry to share, and a message for the world that remains fresh and compelling. For this reason, I draw on insights and experiences from a wide variety of Methodist denominations in Canada and the United States, emphasizing their spiritual common ground.

What follows is a general picture of circuit riders traveling the road to glory. What moved them to heroic efforts and enormous sacrifices in order to make and complete that journey? How did they invite and welcome others to join them? What distractions sent them down dangerous or wasteful side roads? How did they envision and even participate in their destination? What light did their journey shed on the rest of life? How did the road change them over time? How did worship open the floodgates of heaven to renew and empower their work? What difference did they make in shaping society? What resources empowered their traveling? How did they transition from this world to the next? What peculiarities make their work hard for us to understand? How can God use their experience, insights, and actions to inspire and guide us on our own road?

While every time in history has its own distinct challenges and opportunities, the past can offer insights that speak to us today. The heroic era of circuit riding preachers was itself built on Scripture and gathered wisdom from our Wesleyan origins and centuries of inherited tradition. Then, as now, Methodists have found it important and helpful to learn from those sources and apply their learnings to their own situations. It would be strange indeed if the past had nothing of value to offer us in that regard, but in fact, we will find an abundance of connections and applications that can help us navigate the sometimes treacherous waters we face. The great Methodist biographer W.P. Strickland wrote, "History teaches by examples, and without the biographies of those who have been identified with that history we shall be without examples, and fail of the instruction imparted thereby." —W.P. Strickland, *The Life of Jacob Gruber.* New York: Carlton & Porter, 1860, 23.

Even so, what we gain from our past will be less a detailed roadmap than the spiritual foundation, energy, and trajectory for charting our own course. While we can take courage from their successes, and warning from poorly chosen side roads and misadventures, we will need, most of all, spiritual and theological resources for living out our purpose today. We can rejoice in and learn from past voices and victories without imitating precisely the methods and strategies behind them. While there are tragic sins and shortcomings we need to leave behind, there are particulars we need to rediscover, reaffirm, and adapt from their experience. Most of all, we need the Holy Spirit to revive us as he revived them, praying that the One who guided them on their road will guide us on ours.

The Bible itself recognizes the importance of remembering. From Deuteronomy's call to remember God's rescue from Egypt (Deuteronomy 5:15) to Isaiah's cry for exclusive loyalty to God (Is. 46:9), to Jesus' words in the Upper Room (I Corinthians 11:24&25), God calls his people to remember the events of our redemption. Likewise, Scripture warns of the dangers of forgetting. (Deuteronomy 8:19; Psalm 50:22; James 1:22-25) In fact, our remembering reflects God's reliable, complete remembering, something we have always counted on, and forgetfulness like ours is something people have feared might come from God. (Psalm 10:12 &

13:1; Lamentations 5:20) Yet God assures us that, whatever people might do, "I will not forget you!" (Isaiah 49:15, NIV). Again in Isaiah, God says "I have made you, you are my servant; Israel, I will not forget you." (Isaiah 44:21, NIV) In spite of all we have done to make God turn away; in spite of the discipline and punishments we have brought upon ourselves, God says, "I have swept away your offenses like a cloud, your sins like the morning mist." (Isaiah 44:22, NIV)

It is vital that we remember all that God has done for us, and all the ways God has led and commissioned us for his work in the world. Remembering keeps us on track, while forgetting allows us to wander and lose our way. This is specifically true on the road we have traveled as inheritors of the Wesleyan tradition. In spite of homage or lip service paid to the heroism of the past, we have too often walked away from that same past, charting our own courses – often peculiar to each denominational expression. Most often we have exchanged our birthright for something of immediate interest, borrowing from the surrounding culture.

Some may compromise the content and power of worship in order to appeal to a new generation. Others trade the rigors of Christian ethics for the relaxed standards of a selfish and rudderless society. Some have lost interest in the purpose that formed and empowered our Methodist ancestors, discovering new identities with other purposes altogether. Original Wesleyan theology is traded for empty theological trends. Nearly always there is a loss of evangelistic energy. Even where "making disciples of Jesus Christ for the transformation of the world" remains an ostensible mission, there may be little expectation that God will actually transform lives. Changes like these move us closer to a realization of Wesley's fear "lest they should only exist as a dead sect, having the form of religion without the power." —*The Book of Discipline of the United Methodist Church, 2016.* Nashville: The United Methodist Publishing House, 2916, 93; John Wesley, *"Thoughts Upon Methodism," Rupert E. Davies, ed. The Works of John Wesley, Vol. 9.* Nashville: Abingdon, 1989, 527.

Thus, far from being merely a pursuit of irrelevant, antique curiosities, understanding the motivation and spirituality of early Methodist preachers is an essential part of our return to "the path of life." Our tradition, and the larger tradition of the whole of Christianity, is a handing on of living truth from generation to generation. To neglect this handing on amounts to declaring that we have inherited nothing worth taking seriously ourselves or passing on to others. In I Corinthians Paul wrote about Holy Communion as something he "received from the Lord" and then "passed on" to the Church at Corinth. (I Corinthians 11:23, NIV) Later in that book he said he was passing on "as of first importance," the testimony of Christ's resurrection he had received from others and confirmed in his own experience. (I Corinthians 15:3, NIV) As in a relay race, Paul had both received and passed along something of great value, something he knew, or at least hoped, those who received it from him would pass along to others for generations to come. If at any time those future recipients were to lay aside that Tradition and fail to pass it on, they would, by their inaction, tell the world that it no longer mattered. The race, once so faithfully run, would be lost. In that case the Christian road to glory would be replaced by something very different. Are we there yet?

Timothy and Julie Tennent have written a masterful devotion on Psalm 145 that highlights what it means to tradition something from one generation to another. That Psalm testifies to God's goodness, and the urgency of telling the story.

> Many of us became Christians through the testimony and witness of another Christian. The Christian faith has been passed down from person to person for more than two thousand years. We tell the story of the gospel through words and deeds to our children, even as we were told the wonderful story of Christ by those who came before us. It is a remarkable human link, connecting one testimony and changed life with another.

In this way, "One generation will commend your works to another; they will tell of your mighty acts." (Psalm 145:4, NIV) How tragic it is whenever someone or some group within our Christian tradition no longer thinks it important to "contend for the faith that was once for all entrusted to God's holy people." (Jude v. 3, NIV) Likewise, how tragic it is whenever someone or some group within our Wesleyan tradition no longer thinks it important to share the faith that empowered our movement from the beginning – "One generation commending the works of God to another!" —*Timothy and Julie Tennant. A Meditative Journey Through the Psalms.* Franklin, TN: Seedbed, 2017, 214&215.

Included in this tragedy is the neglect of hope for eternal life, a hope shared by everyone in the formative period of our Methodist tradition. What could be more critical than to share God's vision for his people, the purpose and destiny for which we were created? Inseparably linked to this hope is the power of sanctifying grace to "fit us for heaven." —"Away in a Manger," *The United Methodist Hymnal #217, v. 4.* Nashville: Abingdon, 1989. Yet here, too, we often find in our contemporary setting those who shrug spiritual shoulders whenever the conversation goes beyond the "practical" concerns and confines of this life. In this, as in so many things, we must recover the motivating, empowering faith of our Christian and Wesleyan ancestors. Like them we must "tell of the glory of your kingdom and speak of your might, so that all people may know of your mighty acts and the glorious splendor of your kingdom." (Psalm 145:11&12, NIV) As Christians we know the full implications of this, for, "Your kingdom is an everlasting kingdom, and your dominion endures through all generations." (Psalm 145:11-13, NIV) Any redefinition of Christian, Wesleyan faith that omits or downplays sanctification and life beyond death is a hopelessly truncated gospel, really no gospel at all. "If only for this life we have hope in Christ, we are of all people most to be pitied. But Christ has indeed been raised from the dead, the firstfruits of those who have fallen asleep." (I Corinthians 15:19&20, NIV).

We are the inheritors of this amazing news, which was foundational to the beginnings of the Church and the beginnings of Methodism. We will not accept any gospel but the one that "turned the world upside down" and "spread Scripture-holiness over these lands." —Acts 17:6, ESV; Thomas Coke & Francis Asbury. *The Doctrine and Discipline of the Methodist Episcopal Church in America.* Philadelphia: Henry Tuckniss, 1797, iii.

This book gathers the experiences and writings of a broad variety of early Methodist preachers from across North America and from several denominations. The terms "Methodist" and "Wesleyan," unless otherwise indicated, refer to the general movement in which many denominational expressions played a part, even when these terms are not in their names. Each of these expressions is a valued contributor to the larger picture. The stories and insights given here come from across North America, including many from Canada. Each denomination and country has its own experiences and wisdom to share, yet they form a single reality as they unfold the Wesleyan tradition in their own settings. Quoted material remains as in the originals. I have made no attempt to alter the language used by these writers. They need to speak for themselves, in the language of their day, including any expressions that are spelled or arranged differently than we would write them today. I find that what they have to say is very clear and accessible. However, where there is a term than needs clarification, especially where its meaning has changed over time, I will refer to Noah Webster, *An American Dictionary of the English Language.* Springfield, MA: George & Charles Merriam, 1848. Each chapter begins with a pertinent Scripture and words from one of Charles Wesley's hymns.

> "While every advancing year, and revolving day of life shall bring us nearer to a conclusion on earth, let us see also that they ripen us more and more for that state of everlasting quiet, where all shall not only be peace, but joy and assurance for ever." —Laurence Kean, *A Plain and Positive Refutation of the Rev. Samuel Pelton's Unjust and Unfounded Charges, Entitled "The Absurdities of Methodism..."*. New-York: J. and J. Harper, 1823, 6.

Chapter 1

Motivation

"So we fix our eyes not on what is seen, but on what is unseen, since what is seen is temporary, but what is unseen is eternal." —*II Corinthians 4:18, NIV*

"O what delight is this, Which now in Christ we know, An earnest of our glorious bliss, Our heaven begun below!" —Charles Wesley, "O What Delight Is This," *African Methodist Episcopal Hymnal.* Nashville: The Afican Methodist Episcopal Church, 1984, #540, v.1.

Although we may ignore the fact, everyone knows that life in this world is temporary. We long for the eternal (Ecclesiastes 3:11), yet "Change and decay in all around [we] see." —*"Abide with Me," The Hymnal.* Harrisburg, Dayton, Board of Publication of the Evangelical United Brethren Church, 1957, #42, v. 2. One motivation, probably the most powerful one, propelling early Methodists on the road to glory was a realization of life's impermanence, ending universally in death, with no hope beyond death except that "permanent place" promised to "the faithful believer" —Erwin House, *"The Final Home of the Christian Not on Earth but in Heaven," (Sermon) in The Homilist.* New York: Carlton & Porter, 1860, 190.

James Finley set the record straight on the subject of motivation: "Methodist preachers in those days were no sinecures ["an office which has revenue without employment"]. They sought not ease, honor, or popularity; and as far as wealth, that was entirely out of the question. Their hire ["wages"] was souls, and the hope of an eternal reward impelled them onward in the great work in which they were engaged." —W.P. Strickland, ed., *James B. Finley, Sketches of Western Methodism.* Cincinnati: Methodist Book Concern, 1855, 320; Noah Webster, *An American Dictionary of the English Language.* Springfield, MA: George & Charles Merriam, 1848, 554.

Early Methodists, like many other Christians in their day, saw death as sometimes fearful, tragic, and tumultuous, yet often holding the promise of transition to the promised kingdom. Entry into that kingdom was not automatic. The road away from God and life apart from God led to a very different and hopeless end. But heaven was the destination for which God's sanctifying grace was preparing his people, those who freely, and by grace, walked the road to glory. Painful as parting could be, it was not the end of hope, but the door to its full realization. The blessings of God's abundant grace, in and beyond this life, supported people on their journey and kept them moving along the road to glory. (II Peter 1:2)

As Lester Ruth points out, Methodist teachings on eternal life were not unique to themselves, though they were lifted up as foundational to God's plan of salvation.

> Early Methodists' assumptions about the nature of heaven and hell were in line with over a millennium of western Christian teaching on these two realms. Even the disagreements between Protestants and Catholics had concerned less the nature of heaven and hell than the question of who would reside in either realm and why. —Lester Ruth, *Early Methodist Life and Spirituality.* Nashville: Kingswood, 2005, 135.

In other words, Methodist doctrines and preaching on this subject spoke to common concerns of their time. They spoke with special urgency, in part, because of the heartfelt impulse behind their evangelistic outreach. Their passion for souls was linked to an awareness that they were presenting a road and a destiny that, by God's gracious offer, people could actually choose. The call and the power to answer it came from God, but the path required a decision on the part of its travelers.

Echoing this theme about context, Edward Otheman wrote, "There is a broad platform of unsectarian truths upon which, as accountable, dependent beings, we may stand, and say to each other, 'Know the Lord.' We may teach 'Jesus and the resurrection,' as 'the way, the truth and the life,' and no one will reasonably or lawfully object." This context opened doors and hearts for the Methodist message, doors and hearts that in a more secular, skeptical age might well have been tightly closed. —E. Otheman, *Intoduction to James Porter, The Chart of Life: Indicating the dangers and Securities connected with the Voyage to Immortality.* New York: Carlton & Porter, 1854, xv & xvi.

Methodist ideas and commitments regarding heaven and eternal life were based on their own convictions and shared experience, and in turn, on the Bible itself. As Thomas A. Morris put it, "To expect the people to find their way to heaven without the holy Scriptures, is as unreasonable as to require mariners to navigate the high seas without chart or compass." —John F. Marlay. *The Life of Rev. Thomas A. Morris, D.D..* Cincinnati: Hitchcock & Walden; New York: Nelson and Phillips, 1875, 128. Exemplifying this Scriptural foundation is J. Edmondson's Scripture Views of the Heavenly World (New York: Lane & Tippett, 1846), which concludes:

> Men of this world, whose affections are set on things below, would gladly enjoy them for ever; but what are their pleasures worth, in any point of view, when compared with those of the eternal world? Mere earthly pleasures, unconnected with pure and undefiled religion, are worthless; but the pleasures of heaven, which are of incalculable value, demand our most anxious and careful attention. All the things of time are passing away like a rapid flood, and we are carried down by the stream to the vast ocean of eternity; and there our state, whether happy or miserable, will know no change or alteration. ...
>
> A certain prospect of eternal blessedness adds ... joy to every glad heart. There cannot be any fear of death, when the last enemy has been destroyed by the power of Jesus.... Happy spirits, closely united in the bonds of holy friendship, have no painful apprehensions of a separation, for they are all immortal, all fixed firmly on the Rock of ages, and all entitled to the promise of eternal life. (218; 221)

In the meantime, ministry in those early days was extremely hard work, filled with "unremitting toil," but also with "spiritual fervor and downright enthusiasm." United Brethren Bishop W.M. Weekley wrote: "Their labors, sacrifices, and sufferings will never be portrayed by any human tongue, no matter how eloquent, or by any pen, however versatile and fruitful it may be. Footsore and weary, dust covered and battle scarred, they reached the end of their pilgrimage and heard heaven's 'well done.' What a blessed legacy they bequeathed to their sons and daughters in the gospel!" —W. M. Weekley, *Twenty Years on Horseback.* Dayton, OH: United Brethren Publishing House, 1907, 15&16.

William Watters revealed his own motivation when he wrote, "But O! If I could be an instrument in the hands of the Lord Jesus, I bringing dear souls to know him, whom to know is life eternal, it would more than compensate for all my little sufferings in this life, which are but momentary." —William Watters, *A Short Account of the Christian Experience and Min-*

istereal (sic) *Labours of William Watters*. Alexandria, VA: S. Snowden, 1806, 331&32.

Freeborn Garrettson expressed similar thoughts in a letter to John Wesley from Nova Scotia, when he said. "I meet with many difficulties, but a moment's contemplation of the eternal world weighs down all." —Nathan Bangs, *The Life of the Rev. Freeborn Garrettson*. New-York: T. Mason & G. Lane, 1839, 152.

Bishop Joseph Long wrote of financial and other practical hardships among early Evangelical Association preachers:

> A Circuit then extended over the greater part of a state; the country was not infrequently a wilderness with settlements few and far between, which could afford but very poor entertainment 'for man and beast.' The salary ran up all the way from $5.86 to $11.98 a year. Surely it required *a Divine call* to the ministry which was 'as a fire in the bones,' and which caused the young man to exclaim with Paul, 'Woe to me if I preach not the Gospel!' – to brave such adversities and accept such prospects." —R. Yeakel, *Bishop Joseph Long, the Peerless Preacher of the Evangelical Association*. Cleveland: Thomas & Matill, 1897, 11&12.

William Henry Milburn recalled "a word of wholesome counsel given me by an old preacher, as I was starting my career: "Billy, my son, never miss an appointment. Ride all day in any storm, or all night if necessary, ford creeks, swim rivers, run the risk of breaking your neck, or getting drowned, but never miss an appointment, and never be behind the time." —William Henry Milburn, *Ten Years of Preacher-Life*. New York: Derby & Jackson, 1859, 82. To live such a life was to walk in the footsteps of John Wesley, whose preachers were always to "Be punctual. Do everything exactly at the time." After all, theirs was a serious calling, "to save as many souls as you can; to bring as many sinners as you can to repentance, and with all your power to build them up in that holiness without which they cannot see the Lord." —*The Doctrines and Discipline of the Methodist Episcopal Church in America*. Philadelphia, PA: Henry Tuckniss, 1797, 21&22. The same motivation that sent circuit preachers into the North American wilderness, sent missionaries to the far corners of the earth. —See, for example, W.P. Strickland, *History of the Missions of the Methodist Episcopal Church*. Cincinnati: L. Swormstedt & J.H. Power, 1850.

Still, this picture is incomplete; the contrast was not always so stark. Ministry was also filled with excitement, inspiration, and the experience of heaven here and now. Experiences of joy, fellowship, and fulfillment more than balanced poverty, loneliness, and hardship, lightening their burdens and providing what David Adam has called "glimpses of glory." —David Adam, *Glimpses of Glory.* London, UK: SPCK, 2000.

James Horton shared a vision of Christian fellowship that was surely one of those glimpses: "...my soul was so filled with the love of God, and with love to my fellow-men, that I could look on no one without tears gushing from my eyes; each one seemed like an immortal being for whom Christ wept and groaned, bled and died." —James P. Horton. *A Narrative of the Early Life, Remarkable Conversion, and Spiritual Labours of James P. Horton.* n.c.: Printed for the Author, 1839, 24. His words recall the observation of C.S. Lewis, when he recognized that "There are no *ordinary* people." Each person is moving toward an eternal destination. Each person is loved by God, but free to live apart from God. For Lewis, in those who walk the road to glory, "Glory Himself, is truly hidden." —C.S. Lewis, *"The Weight of Glory," in C.S. Lewis. The Weight of Glory and Other Addresses.* Grand Rapids, MI: William B. Eerdmans, 1949, 15. Horton saw something of that glory and it motivated his ministry.

Glory belonged to God. It was and is the nature of heaven. Like the glory revealed in the transfiguration story (Matthew 16:28; Mark 9:1-10; Luke 9:27-36; II Peter 1:16-18), The glory experienced and preached by the circuit riders was dazzling, overpowering, energizing, and revealing. Each experience of glory was a foretaste of God's glorious kingdom. To reach that glory was a major part of what motivated those he called to preach. God shared his glory, as a vision of heaven itself, and as the present experience of heaven come to earth. That experience came in times of prayer, and especially as the high point of Methodist worship. Those who preached that gospel and led that worship saw God's glory as the goal of their journey, experienced that glory along the road, and shared that glory through their ministry. The heavens did not open for preachers alone, but for those who heard them. One woman testified of the preaching of John Johnson, "He talked just like heaven and earth were coming together." After reading countless such accounts, I am convinced that this was not just a simile or exaggeration, but a straightforward description of what often happened in old-time Methodist preaching. Worship at its best was "heaven below." This was not anything the preachers accomplished on their own, but only by the power of the Holy Spirit. —John Berry McFerrin, *History of Methodism in Tennessee, 1818-1840.* Nashville: Southern Methodist Publishing House, 1873, III: 49; Henry H. Knight, III, *Anticipating Heaven Below: Optimism of Grace from Wesley to the Pentecostals.* Eugene, OR: Cascade, 2014.

At the end of their lives, circuit preachers would often share their reflections on the road they had taken, the choices they had made, and whether it had been worth it all. For example, when a colleague asked Thomas Gorsuch "Do you now regret the sacrifices you have made in the ministry?" Gorsuch replied,

> Speak not to me ... about sacrifices; I have made none. I esteem the honor of being permitted to preach the gospel an abundant recompense for any sacrifice I have seemed to make. Oh, the luxury of preaching the gospel. I would willingly take the hardest circuit and the poorest fare if I might once more preach it. Could I live my life over again, and could I foresee all, - the premature decay, the racking pains, this skeletal form, the early grave, —*I'd be a Methodist preacher.* Maxwell P. Gaddis, *Last Words and Old-Time Memories.* New York & Pittsburgh: Phillips & Hunt; Cincinnati & Chicago: Walden & Stowe, 1880, 102.

When Christian Newcomer looked back over eighty years of his life, he remembered, "God's parental care has been with me all the way. He has proven Himself to be a God of love and mercy. Now, in my old age, He feeds my hungry soul with heavenly manna." Looking ahead from that same vantage point, he was "confident that He will aid me by His Spirit, and at last call me home to the bright mansions above, where I shall praise and glorify Him forever." —Samuel S. Hough, ed. *Christian Newcomer.* Dayton: Board of Administration, Church of the United Brethren in Christ, 1941, 15.

Daniel Wise wrote many books designed to instruct young readers in the faith. In one of them he includes chapters on "How to Win Victory in Death" and "Life Beyond the Grave." These include warnings, examples, and appeals that convey the Methodist approach to these subjects in a way that was meant to speak clearly to his readership. In one case, for example, he contrasts the dying experiences of those without faith, who approach the end by steeling themselves against fate, with Christians who approach death much differently. "Do not think," he says, "that in their death such men resemble believers in Christ. There is a distance, almost infinite, between their stoical indifference, and the hallowed peace which reigns in the bosom of a dying believer." In another place he compares the prospects of those who see death as an absolute ending, and those who acknowledge the continuity of eternal life, whether that continuity is positive or negative. For Christians, the trajectory of life includes, for all humanity, two very different paths and destinies. "One of these opposite destinies awaits them all, for there is no middle state for man in eternity. Perfect rest or absolute unrest, everlasting triumph or everlasting despair, heaven or hell, awaits every living soul at the end of the earthly life."

Speaking directly to his young readers, Wise says, "God has made your soul immortal, a 'picture of his own eternity.' Indestructibility is stamped upon it. It is capable, therefore, of enjoying 'everlasting life;' or suffering 'everlasting punishment.' But it cannot be destroyed. Its destiny is to be, to think, to feel, *forever!*" He goes on to say, "This immortality is an attribute of your nature, and invests you with a grandeur which no earth-born greatness can equal...." After a lengthy "tour" of the negative destiny, based on the story of the rich man and Lazarus, Wise attempts to describe the contours of glory. He compares moving from one destiny to another, to "passing from a charnel-house into the pure atmosphere of a bright summer morning." In the positive destiny, all evil and sickness, pain and sin, even death itself, are absent forever. (Revelation 21:4)

> On the other hand there is to be fullness of joy for evermore. God and the Lamb will anticipate and satisfy every want of their nature. Every intellectual aspiration will be gratified in the study of God's infinite being and productions, for they "shall see Him as He is." [I John 3:2] Every desire of the affections shall be met with delightful response, for to them shall be unfolded the meaning of that unfathomed truth, "God is love." [I John 4:16] Every shape of perfect beauty shall charm the eye, and every sound of richest melody shall delight the ear. Read the glorious imagery by which the Revelator vainly sought to convey his impressions of the perfect purity and perfect bliss which he beheld in his inspired visions. —Daniel Wise, *Pleasant Pathways*. New York: Carlton & Porter, 1859, 134; 148; 150; 163; 167&168.

Freeborn Garrettson once offered a shorter version of the choices that must be made regarding eternity and the roads that lead there. It was part of a camp meeting sermon remembered by George Coles, who heard these words: "The memory of that morn, though more than thirty years have since passed away, is as fresh as ever, and the burden of that discourse I shall not soon forget." Garrettson's words were, "Sin makes us ripe for hell! – holiness for heaven!" The impact of these simple words, and the choice they indicate, was magnified by the one who said them and they way he said them: "He had labored in the itinerant field forty-four years, and seemed to stand on the verge of the eternal world; and when he uttered those words, the fullest conviction of their truth glowed in his countenance, sparkled in his eye, appeared in every gesture, and filled the fullest intonations of his voice." —D.P. Kidder, ed., *George Coles, My First Seven Years in America*. New-York: Carlton & Phillips, 1852, 141&142.

Circuit preachers were required to make enormous sacrifices in terms of income, travel, housing, danger, security, health, and family. They worked impossible schedules in order to keep their appointments. They put up with abuse and misunderstanding, and in some cases, intense persecution. What motivated them to choose this kind of life and to see it as a great honor? They saw themselves and their preaching as extensions of God's rescue mission for humanity. They set before individuals and huge assemblies the choice between two eternities, and the opportunity to accept God's offer of salvation, in life and eternity. They were encouraged along the way by glimpses of the heaven they preached, experiences that were shared by their audiences and congregations. They saw themselves as pilgrims on the road to glory, and so they were. Nothing – no detour or diversion – was important enough to rival eternal life as their destination. Every resource; every outpouring of grace, fueled their journey and got them over the inevitable obstacles of temptation and ego. Nothing was so tragic as to lose the way; to exchange one's soul for some transient and ultimately worthless "benefit" offered by this world, for "what do you benefit if you gain the world but lose your own soul?" (Matthew 16:26, NLT) Thus, to Hannah Reeves, "A good meeting to her, where the Holy Spirit attended the word, where sinners were awakened, and saints were joyful in the Lord, was better than all worldly treasures, and pleasures, and honors." —George Brown, *The Lady Preacher.* Philadelphia: Daughaday & Becker; Springfield, OH: Methodist Publishing House, 1870, 153.

Nathan Bangs spoke for his colleagues when he set forth his purpose in ministry: "I am bound for the heavenly city, and my errand among you is to persuade as many as I can to go with me." —Abel Stevens, *Life and Times of Nathan Bangs, D.D.* New York: Carlton & Porter, 1863, 137 *(quoted above, i&ii)*. They were headed for the gloriously transformed existence of heaven, and passionate about sharing that destination with as many as possible.

Chapter 2

Beginnings

"Show me the way I should go, for to you I entrust my life." —*Psalm 143:8, NIV*

"Ye servants of God, your Master proclaim, And publish abroad His wonderful name...." —Charles Wesley, "Ye Servants of God," *The Hymnal*. Harrisburg & Dayton: Board of Publication of the Evangelical United Brethren Church, 1957, #3, v. 1.

Every pilgrimage has a beginning. For Methodist preachers, conversion involved a radical reorientation of their lives, followed at some point by a more specific call into gospel ministry. Each of these milestones would often come amid struggle and self-doubt. The changes required far more than slight adjustments to their accustomed ways of life and work. They set them on a trail leading to a heavenly destiny, and a mission to lead others on that same trail.

Conversions and calls into ministry often followed times of intense turmoil. The father of Alexander Sturgeon Byrne wrote of that time in his son's life, when "he became very anxious respecting his spiritual state; and although we knew it not at the time, for nearly a week immediately preceding his being blessed with pardoning mercy, he was up to a late hour each night wrestling with God in prayer for a revelation of peace to his soul." That turmoil gave way to a new day, when "his countenance glowed with what was expressive of great mental enjoyment...." After being "burdened with a deep sense of guilt, sin, misery, and a need for redemption through a Saviour's blood, I found joy and peace through believing." Soon he could testify to "growing in grace" and experiencing "more peace of mind ... than when I first believed." —John Carroll, *The Stripling Preacher*. Toronto: Anson Green, 1852, 13-15.

Levi Scott's experience was typical, for he approached the possibility of ministry, "Full of painful doubt as to whether it was the will of God that I should become a traveling preacher...." Yet as he later reflected, "The happiest days of my ministry were when I was on a circuit." Each recruit to the itinerancy faced doubt about his own ability, along with a sense of what such a ministry would require. —Levi Scott, in Joseph F. DiPaolo, *Wide Views and a Loving Heart.* Philadelphia: Historical Society of the Eastern Pennsylvania Conference of the United Methodist Church, 2018,16.

Events in John Seybert's early life "temporarily obliterated the pungent convictions he had previously experienced. His advancement towards the kingdom of grace was severely checked, and for the space of three years his religious life was indeed 'A barren waste, and howling wilderness.'" But under the preaching of Matthias Betz, Seybert "received a wound from the sword of the Spirit, and a stroke from the hammer of the Word, from which I never recovered, and the effects of which will continue with me through all eternity. Praise the Lord for it! —S.P. Spreng, *The Life and Labors of John Seybert.* Cleveland, OH: Lauer & Matill, 1888, 24 & 26.

For Freeborn Garrettson it was a moral struggle over the keeping of slaves. Though at that moment he did not understand the issues involved, he was weighed down, unable to function until he realized the source of the problem and freed his slaves. —Nathan Bangs, *The Life of the Rev. Freeborn Garrettson.* New-York: T. Mason & G. Lane, 1839, 39.

George Miller alternated between clarity and being "considerably perplexed" about his call. Even after leaving his old life behind and embarking on itinerancy, he continued to wonder.

> In April, 1805, I started as an itinerant under charge of Jacob Albright and John Walter. At first I was not so clear in my own mind in reference to my call to the ministry, although I was ready to say to the Lord with Isaiah: "Here am I , send me;" and although I had long since felt an inclination to preach the Gospel, from which I might have drawn the conclusion that I was called, like Jeremiah, from my mother's womb, yet this did not and could not satisfy me. I was considerably perplexed. With Paul, I did not wish to run uncertainly, and yet I could find rest in no other way.

What "confirmed [Miller's] calling" was the certainty he gained from actually doing the work of ministry. He wrote,

> *"...before a year had elapsed, all doubt respecting my call was at an end, as well through internal as external evidence; for more than one hundred souls had been saved through my weak efforts, and my conceptions of the Scriptures, which were very indistinct at first, became clearer and clearer through the illumination of the Spirit, so that I could testify to the truth*

with greater clearness and faith.... - God be praised that he did not suffer me to run with uncertainty, but confirmed my calling! —R. Yeakel, *Jacob Albright and His Co-Laborers.* Cleveland: Publishing House of the Evangelical Association, 1883, 199&200.

Ezekiel Cooper chronicled, in great detail, his struggles over whether he should preach:

> My mind became much impressed that it was my duty to warn sinners to "flee from the wrath to come." I suppressed this thought at first, fearing it might not be a call from God. The more I resisted the more I was concerned to publicly declare the counsel of God among men. I used, frequently, to pray in the prayer and class-meetings, and had great happiness in so doing.

Others encouraged Cooper and responded to his exhortations. But preaching would be another matter. He said, "My exercises about preaching increased very fast, until at length they brought about a real distress of soul. I consulted the most experienced friends, and opened my mind to the preachers, both local and traveling. They advised me to make a trial of my gifts." As he was going through all this, Freeborn Garrettson, "under whom I was first of all awakened," was the preacher assigned to his circuit. He gave Cooper an opportunity to serve as a class leader, and in that capacity he "found precious times in meeting the class, the Lord highly favoring us with his presence." But his reluctance to take any further steps continued.

> I still neglected speaking in public as an exhorter or preacher, though a number of friends advised me to take up the cross; but it was so very great to me that I feared and trembled at the thought. At length I felt threatening impressions, as that God would enter into correction if I did not obey – that some judgment would befall me if I refused to do the work appointed by my Master. I feared that my gifts were not adequate to the task; that my abilities were so small and the work so great that I doubted whether I could ever preach the Gospel of God.

Cooper agonized over hearing God clearly calling him. "My uneasiness and anxiety of soul grew to a degree greater than I can describe." He continued to resist, to the point where he says, "I fell into a languishing state of body, and a dull frame of soul. I wore away to a mere skeleton; many thought I would die. I continued in this low condition for several months, being incapable of any business." Yet he could not escape or deny his calling, or the sense that God was punishing him for his unfaithfulness. So he "entered a covenant that if the Lord would restore me to my former state of body and mind, I would preach," with the caveat, "provided I felt the same impressions to it. He tells us that "I began to recover. As my bodily strength returned, my engagedness of soul returned; also my impressions to call upon my fellow-creatures to turn to God." Things had turned a corner for him, and he was able to face and begin exercising his vocation:

> I was now more than ever confirmed in my impression that it was the will of God that I should preach. My concern for souls was very great; my love encircled all mankind; I wanted to see men come home to God. I wept, as it were, between the porch and the altar; watered my pillow by night with tears, and went sorrowing all the day. I thought I could lay down my life, would it prove a means of turning others to the Lord. I was always sorrowing, yet rejoicing, and growing in grace. My peace of soul and love increased....

He could even enter into "altercations upon the truth of the Methodist doctrine," in which "the Lord enabled me to support and prove the truth thereof from Scriptures. It was my constant care to handle all such disputes in mildness and love, and I found it proved much more effectual in convincing and informing the opponents." In view of these experiences, he still resisted preaching itself. After still more anguish over this, "encouraged by one of the preachers with whom I had been for some days, I ventured, after him, one Sabbath, to open my mouth in testimony of the gospel truths." Nor was he speaking only to a small gathering!

> Several hundred were in the assembly.... However, the Lord gave me matter and words to utter his counsel. I spoke again that afternoon ... when I had more liberty, and spoke twice as long. The Lord attended the few hints to several hearts; a number wept considerably. I found great joy and satisfaction in thus submitting to speak for God, though it was not long before I was tempted that I had probably done hurt. However, I again, for a few times, spoke after others of our preachers in different places. I never attempted to have an appointment made for myself, feeling too much diffidence; not at any appointment did I attempt to take a text until I went on the circuit. I believe I never spoke more than eight or ten times, at most, and then after some one else, until ... (Bishop Asbury) prevailed on me to travel.

I include most of this testimony because it so clearly, even painfully, records the genuine experience of this man, and many others, as with great difficulty they came to grips with their call to ministry. Ezekiel Cooper's story is detailed and self-revealing. It takes on special importance when we consider the "He was one of the most eminent among the Methodist fathers, and ... entitled to the veneration of all who love the Methodist Episcopal Church," and in fact the entire movement. —George A. Phoebus, *Beams of Light on Early Methodism in America.* New York: Phillips & Hunt; Cincinnati: Cranston & Stow, 1887, 19-21.

Cooper's testimony was extended and was his own, but it parallels many others. Philip Gatch, another one of the earliest Methodist preachers in America, though opposed by family and friends, continued attending Methodist preaching, but in a confused state. Then,

> …under the deepest exercise of mind, [I] bowed myself before the Lord, and said in my heart, If thou wilt give me the power to call on thy name, how thankful will I be. Immediately I felt the power of God affecting body and soul. It went through my whole system. I felt like crying aloud. God said, by his Spirit, to my soul, "My power is present to heal thy soul, if thou wilt but believe. I felt as if I had got into to new world. I was certainly brought from hell's dark door, and made right with God by the blood of Jesus….

Gatch's "new world" came with the gifts needed to invite and even carry others into that world. When he approached the end of his journey, "His words were received as coming from the verge of mortality….. His biographer, John McLean, wrote that in Gatch's case, as with many others, "They seem nearly connected with the next world, that we can not view them as wholly belonging to earth; and their words are never forgotten. They came to us in the hour of midnight, and are remembered through the whole journey of life." The impact of this man's ministry, culminating in his transition, shed light on the road for others. "In such a life there is safety. The venerable Gatch has mapped out this way. He has so plainly marked it that no one can mistake it. Its end is peace, as all shall find who walk in it." —John M'Lean, *Sketch of Rev. Philip Gatch.* Cincinnati: Swormstedt & Poe, 1854, 13&14; 171; 175.

A young Nathan Bangs, known later for his many accomplishments in ministry, went through a horrific time of spiritual anguish and self-doubt. Abel Stevens' biography of Bangs devotes several pages to this period in his life, which began when he read a popular, eventually discredited attack on the integrity of Methodism. The effect of that book on Bangs and other Methodists in Canada left him questioning everything in his own ministry. "Doubts … crowded around his mind, and enveloped him in utter darkness." He doubted the effectiveness of his work despite considerable evidence to the contrary. He … began to fear that his own spiritual experience had been a delusion." He found it difficult to pray, and in his sleep he was assaulted by demons. He approached preaching "in deep anguish" and when he tried to preach "his heart was 'filled with horrors.'" At one point he "'could hardly stand up; I felt that I ought not to preach, being, as I feared, lost forever.'"

How many preachers, under sufficient pressure, have known similar experiences and have given up. But Bangs persevered, preaching while "'trembling with despair.'" Finally,

> "I returned to the place where I was first seized with this horror, and having a prayer-meeting appointed, I kneeled down and prayed for deliverance. God appeared in gracious power, dispelling the clouds which hung over my mind, removing my doubts and fears, and shining upon my soul with the brightness of his reconciled countenance. All within me rejoiced in God my Saviour." —Abel Stevens, *Life and Times of Nathan Bangs, D.D.* New York: Carlton & Porter, 1863, 87-89.

Nathan Bangs went on to serve with honor, effectiveness, and distinction as one of the best known Methodist preachers, publishers, and authors. His life ended victoriously as, by grace, he made his way on those final steps along the road to glory.

The point of focusing on these struggles is to say that ministry was, in the words of one wedding celebration, "not to be entered into unadvisedly or lightly, but reverently, deliberately, and in accordance with the purposes for which it was instituted by God." Ministry demanded everything from these preachers. —*The Book of Common Prayer.* n.c.: Church Hymnal Corporation & Seabury Press, 1979, 423.

Yet it would be a mistake only to point out the turmoil and difficulties that could accompany someone's calling. Martin Boehm, for example, certainly met with misunderstanding and bewilderment on the part of some who heard him. Before that, he stumbled his way to articulating his experience with God. Farther back still, he agonized over his own salvation. But when it came together for him, Boehm could at last know a joyful ministry. "Like a dream, old things had passed away, and it seemed as if I had awoke to new life, new thoughts, new faith, and new love. I rejoiced and praised God with my whole heart. This joy, this faith, this love, I wished to communicate to those around me...."

His experience, his calling, and his way of expressing it, were not readily accepted by everyone. But toward the end of his life, he could recall his early experience with excitement and joy. Whether others would understand and accept his witness at the beginning, he knew deep within that he had been forgiven, brought close to God, and had a message to preach. He would come to see those around him "rejoicing in the love of God." —Henry G. Spayth, *History of the Church of the United Brethren in Christ.* Circleville, OH: Conference Office, United Brethren in Christ, 1851, 30&31; 35.

For many, entry into faith and ministry involved a radical change of direction and character. Early in James P. Horton's Christian experience, he found his attitudes radically changed from what he had so recently known. "I was sure I had met with a great change, for I used to hate my enemies and I was afraid to die: now I loved my enemies, and the fear of death was gone." The power for such a change came during worship. The direction of that change put him firmly on the road to glory. —James P. Horton. *A Narrative of the Early Life, Remarkable Conversion, and Spiritual Labours of James P. Horton.* n.c: Printed for the Author, 1839, 29.

For most circuit riders, going on the trail meant leaving family, friends, and everything familiar behind. Some were well prepared, but many learned as they went along. Most exchanged the world they had known for one they could only dimly imagine. Many left unchristian attitudes behind, empowered by the Spirit to reflect the moral character of God.

All of them exhibited a hunger for learning. Such was the experience of Peter Cartwright, who "literally gave up the world, and started, bidding farewell to father and mother, brothers and sisters, and met brother Lotspeich [another preacher] at an appointment in Logan County [Kentucky]." There was no time to shadow his partner, let alone attend seminary classes:

> He told me I must preach that night. This I had never done; mine was an exhorter's dispensation. [An exhorter spoke publicly, but in a secondary role.] I tried to beg off, but he urged me to make the effort. I went out and prayed fervently for aid from heaven. All at once it seemed to me as if I could never preach at all, but I struggled in prayer. At length I asked God, if he had called me to preach, to give me aid that night, and give me one soul, that is, convert one soul under my preaching, as evidence that I was called to this work.

The result was astonishing, for him, and for us as we read it·

> The Lord gave light, liberty, and power; the congregation was melted into tears. There was present a professed infidel. The word reached his heart by the Eternal Spirit. He was powerfully convicted, and, as I believe, soundly converted to God that night, and joined the Church, and afterward became a useful member of the same.

Cartwright went on to a lifetime of powerfully effective ministry across several states. He closed his autobiography with a look into a future that was still far off, and said to his readers, "may, O may I meet you all in heaven!" —W.P. Strickland, ed. *Autobiography of Peter Cartwright, the Backwoods Preacher.* New York: Carlton & Porter, 1856, 63&64; 525.

As he looked back over his long ministry, which included fifty years as an itinerant Presiding Elder (District Superintendent), Cartwright said,

> to the young preachers and to the old, that with all the losses and crosses,

labors and sufferings peculiar to the life of a Methodist traveling preacher, I would take, if it was left to my choice, the same track over again with the same religion to bear me up, rather than be President of the United States. Glory to God, there is a religion that sustains a man and will bear him on, and up, and through.

Bishop Thomas Morris rightly said, "there never was but one Peter Cartwright." Yet Cartwright's testimony that his religion had born him "on, and up, and through" the rigors of a long ministry, was mirrored in the reflections of colleagues, as they looked back gratefully on the roads their own ministries had taken. The same power that had brought him liberty and victory in this life, would carry him into glory of eternity. —W.S. Hooper, ed. *Fifty Years as a Presiding Elder, by Rev. Peter Cartwright, D.D.* Cincinnati: Jennings & Graham; New York: Eaton & Mains, 219 & 223.

The joy and glory of ministry more than compensated for its struggles and hardships. Yet that did not make the work easy, or remove its occasional pain. It took the power of God's grace to overcome and work through such things as preachers faced.

We have seen that the call to ministry often led to a period of intense soul-searching, self-doubt, confusion, and inner turmoil. J.N. Brown, for example, says, "As soon as I was converted there was a conviction written upon my soul as with a pen of fire, 'Woe is me if I preach not the Gospel.'" But his initial certainty did not preclude a long struggle:

> I could not escape from this conviction. It followed me night and day, and for three full years I strove against it. Terrible was the conflict, until at last I gave up the struggle, and, laying my all at the feet of Jesus, I promised him that I would go forward as he should open the way, and that I would make it a subject of prayer three times a day until the way should open before me.

The church did not delay in stepping forth to provide a way.

> After I came to this decision, in less than three weeks, without any solicitation on my part, the Church gave me license to exhort. It was wonderful to me. I was poor and weak and unlearned, and I thought that the Church might regard any intimation on my part of such a conviction as a reflection upon the wisdom of God; and now, without waiting for such and intimation, she had recognized my call.

Like other preachers, Brown sought to improve his education for the calling. "I had to struggle through the difficulties of getting an education alone with my own hands without aid from any one except my heavenly Father. It was, indeed a great struggle; but it did me good. It taught me to face difficulties and overcome obstacles, which has been a great help to me in many a trying hour." His initial doubts over, he "filled an honorable sphere and rank among his brethren for forty-five years past." —F.G. Hibbard, *History of the Late East Genesee Conference of the Methodist Episcopal Church.* New York: Phillips & Hunt, 1887, 85&86.

Some early preachers died incredibly early in their ministries, whether from disease, exhaustion, or another cause. Their beginning in this work was also their end. They met their challenge and, sadly, paid a terrible price. Yet their evaluation of this experience could be far different than we might imagine. William Hunt (1787-1810), for example, lived only into his early twenties. But his eye had always been on a kingdom beyond time. Ebenezer F. Newell wrote, "He had worn himself down by travelling and preaching, in hopes of winning precious souls to Christ. In addressing the people, he said , 'Do you ask if I am not sorry for thus exposing myself? I answer, No: and had I ten lives, I would lay them all down in so good a cause." —Abel Stevens, *Memorials of the Early Progress of Methodism.* Boston: C.H. Peirce, 1852, 32&330.

God used Methodism to take people from every kind of background, every type of personality and giftedness, every level of education and experience (or none), from every arena of North American culture, and worked in them to produce powerful witnesses for Christ and leaders for the church. Whatever form of Methodism they came from or worked in, regardless of ethnicity or customs or preferences, God found ways for them to fulfill his vision for their lives and the lives of those for whom and with whom they served. It was not easy to accept the challenge and sacrifice of a life on this road to glory, and there certainly was no reward of the kind usually associated with any kind of employment. But this was a life lived for eternal reasons, with an eternal destiny in view, for themselves and those they served. Many found the opportunity to seek the kingdom, and to call others into that same kingdom, worth whatever the cost might be.

CHAPTER 3

Expectation

"We are therefore Christ's ambassadors, as though God were making his appeal through us." —*II Corinthians 5:20, NIV*

"To serve the present age, My calling to fulfill; O may it all my powers engage To do my Master's will!" —Charles Wesley, "A Charge to Keep I Have," *The African Methodist Episcopal Church Hymnal.* Nashville: The African Methodist Episcopal Church, 1984, #242, v. 2.

There was no bait and switch in the call to ministry in the Methodist tradition. The life of a preacher, especially an itinerant, took everything that person had to give. There was, however, a clarity of purpose, a call from God that made every sacrifice worthwhile. James Porter wrote that anyone suited to the rigors of itinerant ministry must be someone 'whose convictions of duty disallow of their pursuing any thing else." Among the many specific qualifications for this work: "They must be men … who are really converted to God … and heirs of heaven." It was essential for them to be "saving souls from death." Thus, whatever other considerations came into play, a Methodist preacher must be proficient in "the arithmetic of future things, the profit and loss of a soul to all eternity." —James Porter, *The True Evangelist.* Boston: Waite, Peirce and Company, 1847. Porter knew how precarious this life can be, as when Charles Wesley wrote,

> A point of time, a moment's space, Removes me to that heavenly place, Or shuts me up in hell.

Yet for preachers in our tradition, even life "on a narrow neck of land, 'Twixt two unbounded seas," focused on hell only long enough to put and keep people on the road to heaven,

> Where faith is sweetly lost in sight, and hope, in full supreme delight, And

everlasting love. —Charles Wesley, *"Lo! On a Narrow Neck of Land,"* in *The Tribute of Praise.* Pittsburgh: U.S. Fleming & Baltimore: W.J.C. Dulany (Methodist Protestant Publishing House, 1882, #421, vs. 1&5.

From the beginning, the expectations placed upon ministers in the Wesleyan tradition were exacting and strenuous. Essential duties of a preacher included, first and foremost, preaching, at whatever time of day a congregation could be brought together. The preacher must also "meet the societies, classes, and bands." A preacher must "Be diligent. Never be unemployed; never be triflingly employed. Never trifle away time; neither spend any more time at any place than is strictly necessary." That minister must "Be serious." Time must be given to "visiting from house to house: in reading, meditation, and prayer." All of this was to be done while traveling, without sufficient income and as a guest of anyone willing to extend hospitality. "And remember! A Methodist preacher is to mind every point, great and small, in the Methodist discipline! Therefore you will need to exercise all the sense and grace you have." —*The Doctrines and Discipline of the Methodist Episcopal Church in America.* Philadelphia: Henry Tuckniss, 1797, 22. Similar instructions and requirements were given for preachers in other Wesleyan bodies, such as the United Brethren in Christ. —*Origin, Doctrine, Constitution and Discipline of the United Brethren in Christ.* Dayton: Printing Establishment of the United Brethren in Christ, 1859, 45-48. A portion of the expectations given to Canadian Wesleyan preachers by the 1836 Discipline reads:

> We advise you, 1. As often as possible to rise at four. 2. From four to five in the morning, and from five to six in the evening, to meditate, pray, and read the Scriptures with notes, and the closely practical parts of what Mr. Wesley has published. From six in the morning till twelve, (allowing an hour for breakfast) read, with much prayer, some of our best religious tracts. ... 1. Read the most useful books, and that regularly and constantly. 2. Steadily spend all the morning in this employment, or at least five hours in four and twenty. "But I have no taste for reading." Contract a taste for it by use, or return to your former employment. "I have no books." Be diligent to spread the books, and you will have use of them. —*The Doctrines and Discipline of the Wesleyan Methodist Church in Canada.* Toronto: Matthew Lang, 1836, 56&57.

The life of an early preacher in the Wesleyan tradition, especially on the frontier, was most often hard, dangerous, and poorly paid. Pioneer preachers were never far from the elements and the uncertainties of the road, but often far from home and family. Thomas Coke was clear on the ultimate purpose that made it all worthwhile:

...God, in all the trials and afflictions which he lays upon or suffers to happen to his zealous ministering servants, has but two ends in his view and in his gracious intention: first, their sanctification and eternal happiness: secondly, their usefulness in the Church. Everything he permits or does for them here below, he does it, or permits it, only to facilitate these gracious designs: every agreeable or afflictive event which in any way concerns them, he has prepared for them, to make them more holy, useful, and eternally glorious.

After all, in Coke's view and that of Methodism generally, "All this visible world itself was only made for the world which is to come: all that passes here has its secret connection with eternity: all that which we see is only a figure of things invisible." Because so much was at stake, for preachers and their audiences alike, "It is not your [the preacher's] business only to preach so many times, and to take care of this or that society, but to save as many souls as you can." —Thomas Coke, *"Four Discourses on the Duties of a Minister of the Gospel,"* in Adam Clarke and Thomas Coke, *The Preacher's Manual.* Nashville: Publishing House of the M.E. Church, South, 1889, 256, 257; 215.

Coke's principle was echoed by circuit preacher Benjamin Young, who after explaining his great poverty, said, "But I trust I am in the way to heaven, and I know my heart is engaged in the work of God." —Abel Stevens, *History of the Methodist Episcopal Church.* New York: Carlton & Porter, 1867, 154.

It was the expectation of every preacher, confirmed constantly in practice, that he or she would offer people the gift of hope, rooted in the nature of eternal life. That hope involved not only a personal destiny, but a destiny that carried relationships of love known in this world, into the next.

> Happy spirits, closely united in the bonds of holy friendship, have no painful apprehensions of a separation; for they are all immortal, all fixed firmly on the Rock of ages, and all entitled to the promise of eternal life. Here we live awhile in friendship; but when death comes, we lose our friends, and mourn like the dove: but this cannot happen in a world of life, where every friend with whom we may associate is placed far beyond the bounds of mortality. —J. Edmondson, *Scripture Views of the Heavenly World.* New-York: G. Lane & C.B. Tippett, 1846, 221.

Jesus' mission in the world was to turn us around and renew us in God's image, so that, through grace, we would "participate in the divine nature." (II Peter 1:4, NIV) That nature is eternal. God is eternal, "'from everlasting to everlasting,' unchangeably the same. Psa. xc, 2." Heaven is eternal, and we are set on the road to heaven's eternal glory.

This [eternal life] is the highest state of perfection; and without it nothing is perfect. ...; but infinite perfection, connected with eternal duration, is the glory of the divine nature. And immortality will be the glory of created excellence, which, though infinitely inferior to that of God, will resemble him in its eternal duration. —J. Edmondson, *Scripture Views of the Heavenly World.* New-York: G. Lane & C.B. Tippett, 1846, 222.

This assurance, in the life of a preacher and in the heart of the message, gave undying hope and purpose to life and salvation. Every preacher worked under the auspices and from the perspective of eternity. No decision or action could any longer be viewed as inconsequential for each one participated in the trajectory of one's life. Each moral or vocational choice was directed either to heaven, or to hell. Even the emptiness of triviality to which so much of life is unfortunately given partakes of hell because it seeks nothing better. That is why there was so much at stake in someone's calling into ministry. That call, together with its acceptance and fruition, had consequences for the one who received it, and for everyone who would ever be influenced by that person's preaching, counsel, leadership, and example. Most important of all would be the consequences of taking, or rejecting, the road to glory.

For John McLean, writing of the ministry of Philip Gatch,

To be a Methodist preacher is to live a life of labor, whether local or traveling. Those who travel circuits are exposed to all sorts of weather, different diet, and lodging; besides preaching they attend to the societies and other arduous duties. The local preachers, too, have to labor, like other men, six days in the week, and on the Sabbath to preach, which exhausts their physical power more than labor; but their reward is with the Lord. —John M'Lean, *Sketch of Rev. Philip Gatch.* Cincinnati: Swormstedt & Poe, 1854, 119.

John Carroll echoed this theme as he wrote of the total commitment expected of preachers and lay people alike: "The Wesleyan Church [referring to the Wesleyan Church in Canada, but appropriate to all the Wesleyan bodies], constructed on the model of the primitive one, feels that she needs the exercise of every particle of available talent in her members, in carrying out her plans of aggression on the kingdom of darkness...." —John Carroll, *The Stripling Preacher, or a Sketch of the Life and Character ... of the Rev. Alexander S. Byrne.* Toronto: Anson Green, 1852, 17&18.

George Coles wrote of his reaction to a "dreadful north-wester coming up from the river and the valley...." He said, "I felt as if I should like to return home. But I had no home to go to, and perhaps it was well I had not; for if only one soul is saved by my humble instrumentality, and I get safe to heaven at last, eternity will make amends for all." —George Coles, *My First Seven Year in America.* New-York: Carlton & Porter, 1852, 64.

The grandeur of heaven and the eternal implications of our life on earth were regular themes in early Methodist preaching, but more than that, they were key motivating factors in the lives of those who preached them. John Lewis Dyer wrote that in the New Testament, "Christ describes the torments of hell and the glories of heaven and eternal happiness." Therefore it is incumbent on Methodist preachers to hold both possibilities before their congregations. "This is the call, and any preacher who leaves out half is unfaithful to it...." But the hope was always for final salvation, the good and beautiful destiny of eternal life in the heavenly kingdom. —*John Lewis Dyer. The Snow-Shoe Itinerant.* Cincinnati: Cranston & Stowe, 1890, 202.

Thus, the expectations inherent in a call to ministry, or an appointment to a given circuit or station, serve this overarching purpose. The implication of all this, difficult or impossible as it could be under practical circumstances, which often provided inadequate financial support, was that those who engage in the rigors of itinerant ministry must be those "whose convictions of duty disallow of their pursuing any thing else." To do this, they required strong enough motivation to get them through any challenge or obstacle to their ministry.

Thomas Coke, driven along his own road to glory by these same expectations, traveled relentlessly across Britain, Ireland, and North America – especially the West Indies. As if that were not enough, he died on his way to India.

Always there remained a balance, well expressed in the hymn "Come Let Us Anew," where we live our Christian lives "By the patience of hope, and the labor of love." —Charles Wesley, *"Come Let Us Anew," in The Tribute of Praise.* Pittsburgh: U.S. Fleming & Baltimore: W.J.C. Dulaney (Board of Publication of the Methodist Protestant Church), 1882, #554, v. 1.

Chapter 4

Invitation

"…you will be my witnesses … to the ends of the earth." —*Acts 1:8, NIV*

"And gladly reckon all things loss so we may Jesus gain." —Charles Wesley, "And Are We Yet Alive," *The United Methodist Hymnal.* Nashville: The United Methodist Publishing House, 1989, #553, v. 6.

Nathan Bangs introduced himself to a community in Upper Canada (Ontario) he had been appointed to serve. As part of his introduction/testimony, he said, "I am bound for the heavenly city, and my errand among you is to persuade as many as I can to go with me." This was a large part of his reason for the "long and tedious journey" that had taken him from New York to this new assignment. Much later, as he was dying, he could see the approach of his destination. "The presence of Jesus lights up my room. It has lighted up the entire way to heaven. My way is clear." After inviting many to join him, he was himself ready to enter "the heavenly city." This life of invitation and arrival was common to preachers of his time, and central to all they accomplished in ministry. This life was never their "final destination," but instead served as their road to glory. —Abel Stevens, *Life and Times of Nathan Bangs, D.D.* New York: Carlton & Porter, 1863, 137; Maxwell Pierson Gaddis, *Last Words and Old-Time Memories.* New York & Pittsburgh: Phillips & Hunt; Cincinnati & Chicago: Walden & Stowe, 1880, 15&16.

Preachers in the Wesleyan tradition expected to change both individuals and society; to impact this world and the next. Robert Tuttle highlighted the Evangelical and United Brethren contribution – what he called "The Otterbein/Albright Models" - to bringing this world under God's rule: Jacob Albright, for example, sought revival and sanctification "among the Germans in America" so as "to bring them again to the true life of godliness, so that they, too, might become partakers of the blessed peace with God and the fellowship of the saints in light." At the same time, German Evangelicals and United Brethren shared "an emphasis upon sanctification which included a deep social witness. For example, as part of their teaching on holiness, both the United Brethren and the Evangelical Association stood unanimously opposed to slavery, child labor, and the abuse of alcohol and tobacco." —Robert Tuttle, *On Giant Shoulders*. Nashville: Discipleship Resources, 1984, 75 & 87.

Enlisting people into such a life was often a matter of example, but also of an inner calling that could not be ignored. John Stewart tried his best to run away from God's call on his life, a call that was to take him to northeastern Ohio, to minister to the Wyandotte Indians.

At one point, "being one evening at private devotion, suddenly he heard a sound which much alarmed him: as a voice (as he thought) said to him – 'Thou shalt declare my counsel faithfully....'" But the call was more specific:

> ...at the same time a view appeared to open to him in a Northwest direction, and a strong impression was made on his mind, that he must go out that course into the world to declare the counsel of God. This singular event gave him much uneasiness and exercise of mind, and having mentioned the matter to a friend, he received an explanation which greatly increased his concern; for it was intimated that he might expect to be called upon to go abroad and preach the gospel which to him was an afflicting consideration, having never before considered such an undertaking. Judging himself entirely unqualified for such a work, he determined to avoid it if possible, and accordingly made ready to follow his friends to the State of Tennessee.

Like many, however, John Stewart could not escape his call. A serious illness prevented his travel south, and the call continued to haunt him.

> He still fancied he heard sounding in his ears the voice above mentioned, and the same impression continued with respect to his travelling to the Northwest. At length he resolved, that if it should please the Lord to spare his life, and restore him to health again, he would go out that course and see where he would be conducted, although he feared he should be killed by the first Indians he should meet with. He was restored to health, and according to the determination he had entered into before his God, he set out without credentials, directions of the way, money or bread, crossed the Muskingum River for the first time, and travelled a northwest course, "not knowing whither he went."

Discouraging factors continued to block Stewart's way, but this time, discouraged though he might be, he stuck tenaciously to his resolve. "As he proceeded he was met by sundry persons, who, having learned something of the nature of his undertaking, strove in vain to dissuade him from the pursuit. He urged on his way, keeping about the same course, which he was frequently informed would lead him into the Indian country on the Sandusky river," eventually meeting some of the Indians he had feared, but who actually welcomed him, though neither spoke the other's language. Stewart became the pioneering preacher for what became the Wyandotte Mission, in which James Finley, Jacob Young, and others would also play a part. As unlikely – and unwelcome – as his specific calling seemed, it eventually led to effective ministry. —*The Missionary Pioneer ... John Stewart.* New-York: J.C. Totten, 1827, 15-17.

Another invitation story comes from the Methodist work among Mississauga indigenous people in Upper Canada. When Peter Jones (Kahkewaquonaby) first spoke to his fellow Mississauga John Sunday (Shawundais) about Christianity (1826), he told him, "All individuals ... Aboriginal and non-Aboriginal, travelled down one of two roads: 'The broad road that leads to destruction, and the narrow road that leads to heaven.'" The idea of a path leading to "everlasting fire" terrified Shawundais. When Jones visited him a second time, he...

> ...asked Shawundais to pray in Ojibwe. He did so, saying only, 'O Keshamunedo, shahnanemeshin' (O Lord have mercy on me poor sinner.) Then it happened. Those few Ojibwe words led Shawundais to shout and shake with joy: 'I feel something in my heart.' Peter Jones replied, 'The Lord blesses you now.'

A few months later, Sunday joined Jones and another recent convert "on a missionary tour to Lake Simcoe. Methodist missionary William Case worked with them and others until "Almost all the Mississauga in the Belleville area [their home region, in Upper Canada] entered the Methodist Church, 130 individuals." More conversions followed. When Jones first told Sunday about the two roads, he was not encouraging Sunday to *earn* salvation, but rather to set out, *through* the grace he had received in salvation, on "the narrow road that leads to heaven." Sunday, and many others afterwards, took these words, ultimately the words of Jesus, seriously, and wasted no time before starting and walking down that road. This was the invitation Jones gave to Sunday, who accepted it and passed it on. —Donald B. Smith, *Mississauga Portraits. T*oronto, Buffalo, & London: University of Toronto Press, 2013, 222-223.

The invitation might be this specific, but it could also be very general. Once the calling had been accepted, some preachers were ready to go wherever they might be sent, even if it meant significant travel. An initial appointment would lead to others, so that rootlessness became for many a way of life. In John Stewart's case, the absence of money, language skills, education, and the fact that he had "never before considered such an undertaking," all yielded to complete dependence on grace, often expressed through strangers and circumstances he could not have imagined.

Orange Scott wrote of his first steps in ministry, saying,

> "I knew ... that I had little or no qualifications, except sincerity and the love of God. Yet I felt that if God called me into the work, he would support and sustain me in it. I was willing to glorify God in this way, if I could be persuaded, it was his will." Accordingly, about the first of November, 1821, he started on foot for Barnard circuit, distant forty miles. He had no books but the Bible, and a hymn book; no clothing, but what was on his back, and in a small portmanteau ["A bag usually made of leather, for carrying apparel and other furniture on journeys, particularly on horseback."]; no companion or friend, and in debt $30. "Thus," he remarks, "commenced my course of brilliant (!) exploits as a poor itinerant Methodist preacher." —Lucius C. Matlack, *The Life of Rev. Orange Scott.* New York: C. Prindle & L.C. Matlack, 1847, 59; Noah Webster, *An American Dictionary of the English Language.* Springfield, MA: George & Charles Merriam, 1848, 848.

Scott's considerable gifts, thirst for learning, and complete dedication became the tools of grace for his career, but without even a horse, this was a painfully difficult beginning.

Jarena Lee would embark on her ministry with even less, since as a woman she could not be ordained or licensed in her denomination (or most others). Bishop Richard Allen gave her a letter commending her ministry, and her reputation would draw congregations, but she had no official credentials and few resources to support what she was doing. Often she had to walk from one preaching engagement to another. Of one segment of her life she said,

> I have travelled, in four years, sixteen hundred miles and of that I walked two hundred and eleven miles, and preached the kingdom of God to the falling sons and daughters of Adam, counting it all joy for the sake of Jesus. Many times cast down but not forsaken; willing to suffer as well as love."

Sister Lee often felt called upon to justify her ministry, for though several women preached within smaller Methodist denominations at that time, they were few and scattered across the continent. She was unwilling to allow "that holy energy which burned within me ... to be smothered." So she preached at every opportunity, knowing and feeling the resistance of much of the Church:

For as unseemly as it may appear now-a-days for a woman to preach, it should be remembered that nothing is impossible with God. And why should it be thought impossible, heterodox, or improper for a woman to preach? seeing the Saviour died for the woman as well as for the man.

If the man may preach, because the Saviour died for him, why not the woman? seeing he died for her also. Is he not a whole Saviour, instead of a half one? as those who hold it wrong for a woman to preach, would seem to make it appear.

She also pointed to the fruits of her ministry as validating her calling: "As for me, I am fully persuaded that the Lord called me to labor according to what I have received, in his vineyard. If he has not, how could he consistently bear testimony in favor of my poor labors, in awakening and converting sinners?" —Jarena Lee, *Religious Experience and Journal of Mrs. Jarena Lee*. Philadelphia: Printed and Published for the Author, 1849, 36; 10-12.

The Invitation to preach the Gospel, whether in general or to a specific audience, was clear, compelling, and empowered by the Spirit of God. There was affirmation from individuals and churches, but there were also obstacles, especially for women and people of color. There were encouraging results, which spoke to the pragmatic nature of the revival and the Methodist movement. There were sacrifices, and there were spiritual rewards greater than those sacrifices. Ultimately what was at stake was the destiny of preacher and people alike, for "how can they believe in the one of whom they have not heard? And how can they hear without someone preaching to them?" (Romans 10:14, NIV).

CHAPTER 5

Distraction

"Better is one day in your courts than a thousand elsewhere...." —*Psalms 84:10, NIV*

"To Thee with my whole soul aspire; Dead to the world and all its toys...." —Charles Wesley, "Come, Holy Ghost, All-Quickening Fire," *Hymns of Faith and Life.* Winona Lake, IN: Light and Life Press & Marion; IN: Wesley Press, 1976, #320, v.3.

Distractions, even in those relatively simple times, everywhere sought to weaken a Methodist's faith by offering alternatives to those occupations of mind and heart which would both support and express the pilgrim journey. As with the earlier time of the Wesleys, there were attitudes and activities that were inconsistent with a Christian's profession and capable of leading someone off course, either temporarily or forever.

In his introduction to James Porter' *The Chart of Life*, E. Otheman cautions us with these words: "Reader, you are on the dangerous voyage of life, bearing the inestimable freight of immortal destiny; all your hopes of endless joy depend upon the course you steer." And again he asks, "How many an immortal spirit is ... heedless of its destiny. Reader, are you aware for what end you live?" —E. Otheman, *Introduction to James Porter, The Chart of Life.* New York: Phillips & Hunt; Cincinnati: Walden & Stow, 1883, xiv.

Thus Wesley's General Rules delineated many things that, while antithetical to the Methodist vision of life and eternity, were nonetheless popular and difficult to root out. The point was "doing no harm, by avoiding evil of every kind; especially that which is most generally practiced...." Included in the list were "taking the name of God in vain," improper use of Sunday as Sabbath; drunkenness, fighting and taking revenge; smuggling;

and "*Uncharitable* or *unprofitable* conversation…; Doing to others as we would not they should do unto us: Doing what we know is not for the glory of God," and so on. With this list were two others, one for "avoiding evil of every kind," and the other to promote faithfully taking part in private and public worship. —*A Form of Discipline*. Philadelphia: Aitken & Son, 1790, 46-48.

To monitor Methodists' progress in these, class meetings (though originally developed for other purposes) brought people into small groups, led by class leaders, to look into the faithfulness of their members in these important means and evidences of grace. Class leaders, working locally, but in cooperation with traveling preachers, were "to see each person in their several classes once a week at least, in order to inquire how their souls prosper; not only how each person observes the outward rules, but how he grows in the knowledge and love of God." —John Miley, *Treatise on Class Meetings*. Cincinnati: Methodist Book Concern, 1851, 55. This purpose is drawn largely from II Peter 3:18, where each Christian is urged to "grow in the grace and knowledge of our Lord and Savior Jesus Christ. To him be glory both now and forever! Amen." (II Peter 3:18, NIV) The ultimate purpose, in other words, is not merely small group discipline and coordination, but providing a framework for sanctification to unfold in peoples' lives. The point was that distractions were not only morally or spiritually sinful, destructive, or at least empty and meaningless. They were what modern day Walk to Emmaus calls "obstacles to grace," diametrically opposed to the means of grace Wesley detailed.

In the pioneering days of the Wesleyan movement in North America, preachers and others complained of intemperance, gambling, ostentation in dress, conspicuous consumption, certain forms of public entertainment, rough and tumble fighting, and preoccupation with selfish concerns. Converts turned away from such things as a function of their new spiritual life and the demands of discipleship, often lamenting these past sins because of the time and energy they had wasted and the damage they had caused. John Lewis Dyer, working in the mining camps of Colorado, would boldly interrupt card games to invite players to do something more important, which was to attend preaching – often with success! He believed that dancing was perhaps the most dangerous of all distractions because in his experience it encouraged promiscuity and infidelity. On the other hand, he benefited from the misguided but well-intentioned efforts of a local man who recruited a congregation from within a saloon – by buying rounds! —John Lewis Dyer, *The Snow-Shoe Itinerant: An Autobiography*. Cincinnati: Cranston & Stowe, 1890, 142; 156&157; 264&265; 248&249.

Also of serious consequence were social and political distractions; issues and events important in themselves, yet diverting attention from the central purpose of the movement. Among these were authority and organization within the churches, war between nations, anti-Catholicism, and growing affluence.

Almost from the beginning of the Methodist Episcopal Church, there were movements whose aim was to change or modify the way appointments were made and leadership selected within the church. James O'Kelly's Republican Methodists, the Methodist Protestant Church, the Wesleyan Methodist Connexion, and the Free Methodist Church, all began, at least in part, with efforts to reform the parent body. Other issues, especially slavery, were even more important to the Wesleyans and Free Methodists, but church organization and politics brought all of them to a point of conflict and separation. In situations where slavery and discrimination were the main issue, these serious ethical matters resulted in the formation of the African Methodist Church and the African Methodist Episcopal Zion Church. Radically opposed views on how Christians should think and act on slavery divided the Methodist Episcopal Church in much the same way they came to divide the United States. While Canada took an earlier antislavery position, Canadians continued to live with racial discrimination and tensions, often related to issues of social and economic class, and bringing about the extension of African Methodism into the country, and the birth of the British Methodist Episcopal Church among those who had safely arrived via the Underground Railroad.

Some of these conflicts could not be avoided without compromising both the gospel and the nature of Methodism. Others concerned more peripheral matters that did not strike at the heart of the faith. But in every case, whenever such conflict and division took place, the issues involved often replaced or competed with the spiritual purpose of Methodism as the main concern. This is clear in the histories of each group, in which the causes of separation and continuing differences take center stage. The case of slavery and racial prejudice was by far the most significant and divisive of all contentious matters before the churches, dramatically impacting people's lives and crying out for a Christian perspective and resolution that remain incomplete. Slavery in turn led to the Civil War, which tore the American nation apart and left it badly divided.

Because equality and antislavery were part of the original Wesleyan movement, in England and North America, the conflicts which surrounded them were not merely a distraction or an internal matter, but a challenge to the nature of Methodism (and Christianity) itself. So deep and extensive was this challenge that it became impossible for some of the Methodist bodies to come to any sort of agreement. Beyond that, approval of or compromise with slavery could not be maintained, in any section of the continent, without calling into question fundamental commitments of Wesley and primitive Methodism on this side of the Atlantic. Attempts within the M.E. Church to reach a compromise only drove the antagonists farther apart.

There can be no question that slavery, as a moral and cultural issue, diverted attention from evangelism and holiness. Support for slavery undermined Christianity itself. While subsequent history has brought us to the point where slavery and racism are universally condemned, it was too early for that kind of transformation in some preachers and people of the early nineteenth century.

As the century wore on, matters of faith and national/cultural identity merged in the thinking of many. Christianity and culture moved together to bring the world to what all hoped would be a better place. Ideas of a Christian America, with "Christian" meaning evangelical Protestant, occupied the pens and pulpits of the country. A similar, though not as bellicose, pattern could be seen in Canada, though Canada's demographics, the special case of Quebec, and status within the British Empire, created its own distinctive ethos.

For many in the United States, issues of war and jingoistic nationalism stood well apart from Christian identity, even as others would see participation in or support of a given war as an expression of their faith. It was obvious for some that matters of war between nations must be seen as similar to conflict between individuals, and could not be tolerated among ostensibly Christian nations. Some voices lamented the way war distracted people, churches, and communities from the main business of revival and reform. Some raised concern about what they saw as spiritual conflict between the gospel and the spirit and effects of war itself, or a particular war.

Concerning the spiritual results of the War of 1812, Charles Giles wrote,

> ...we had been greatly annoyed in our religious operations by the civil commotions in the country, and especially throughout the northern part of the conference, along the troubled line [the U.S.-Canadian border], where the elements of ambition and revenge were continually raging. As a natural consequence, the public mind was kept in a state of agitation, and many growing societies were reduced and distracted in these evil days. So the distressing and demoralizing effects and influences growing out of that disastrous war were felt everywhere, and did unavoidably impede the prosperity of our community. Hence, when the proclamation came in, that our national difficulties were settled, it awakened emotions of gratitude

and delight in all our hearts; and it was our ardent desire never to see the church or nation troubled again with such needless calamities. —Charles Giles, *Pioneer.* New-York: G. Lane & P.P. Sandford, 1844, 220.

This distraction was most strongly felt in border conferences, including the Genesee Conference of the Methodist Episcopal Church, which included churches and pastors in both countries. Abner Chase left this reflection from a time when he was in Canada for annual conference in 1820:

> After crossing the [Niagara] river ... we were overtaken by a man on horseback, having the appearance of a gentleman, who accosted us very pleasantly, and after a few remarks respecting the steepness of the rocks which bounded the shore, he remarked, "it was a d---- funny sight to see the Yankees driven down that ledge." Suddenly as an electric shock there came over me a feeling which I would not have retained one day for a world. It was such as I supposed men sometimes feel when they are, insulted, and are disposed to seek revenge; and I thought of cannon, muskets, swords, and retaliation. But this sudden impulse passed away almost as suddenly as it came, and I felt only pity instead of revenge.

> After ascending these heights, a few miles' ride brought us to the entrance of the far-famed Lundy's Lane, the scene of the hottest, and for the members engaged, the most bloody battle fought during our last war with Great Britain. We took a particular survey of the little eminence which was the rallying point in that battle, and which I think we were told was taken and retaken nine times during the battle, at the point of the bayonet. What multitudes "bit the ground in death" on that awful night! fallen by a brother's hand. Their bones now lay quietly commingling in strange confusion, and but partially concealed, many of them were bleaching in winter snows and summer showers and sun. ... But why should such scenes desolate the earth in these enlightened ages and nations? We can offer some apology for poor fallen humanity in the days and regions of heathen barbarism: but why should the two most enlightened and Christianized nations upon the earth still perpetuate this barbarous custom, and butcher each other for supposed or real wrongs. Surely there must be a more consistent and Christian mode of deciding a controversy between nations as well as individuals, than an appeal to the sword. —Abner Chase, *Recollections of the Past.* New-York: Conference Office, 1846, 134-136.

James B. Finley made this observation about the issue in his autobiography:

> This year the war spirit unfortunately entered into many professors of religion, and as soon as they caught it they began to lose their religion. Many that once walked with us to the house of God and took delight in the services of religion, now marched off in rank and file to become disciplined

in the arts of war. Several, who had been saved from drunkenness by the Church, returned to their evil habits as "the dog returns to his vomit, and the sow, that was washed, to her wallowing in the mire." Wars and rumors of wars are peculiarly fatal to the mild and peaceful spirit of the Gospel; and when the Prince of peace shall obtain his dominions, "swords shall be beaten into plowshares and spears into pruning-hooks, and nations shall learn war no more." —W.P. Strickland, ed., *Autobiography of Rev. James B. Finley.* Cincinnati: Methodist Book Concern, 1855, 259.

Jacob Young wrote about the way the War of 1812 distracted people, saying, "The people were so much taken up with war and politics, that they lost their zeal in the cause of God." He told the story of one camp meeting where a "commanding officer" requested that "the soldiers might be addressed by one of the ministers" prior to a planned march to engage with the British. Bishop Asbury agreed to speak to them; Young summarized the bishop's words.

> In his introductory remarks he dwelt clearly on the great evils of war - its deleterious influence on the commerce and wealth of nations, but more so on the religious morals and happiness of nations; and that it ought to be avoided, if possible - that a declaration of war should be the last resort - that all other suitable means should be tried previous to war; and, that, if Christian nations went to war, it should always be on the defensive. ... [Following the sermon,] He laid his hand on the head of the commanding officer - prayed for him devoutly, and gave him fatherly advice - tears flowed abundantly. The Bishop stood there till he shook hands with every soldier in the company.
>
> They all marched away - many of the poor fellows never returned again. — Jacob Young, *Autobiography of a Pioneer.* Cincinnati: Cranston & Curts; New York: Hunt & Eaton, n.d., 309; 292-294.

William Hanby, a bishop in the United Brethren Church, wrote of the spiritual damage and distraction brought on by the Mexican War:

> During this year [1847], the whole nation was immersed more or less, in the spirit of war. A bloodly [sic] war was kept up between the United States and Mexico, in which harder battles were fought, and perhaps more lives lost, than in the American revolution.
>
> This state of things affected materially the interest of Zion. Recruiting officers were found in all the towns and villages from Maine to Georgia, on week day and Sunday beating up for volunteers. The Church, to a very great extent, drank in the same spirit. Many church members, and even officers, such as leaders, exhorters, stewards, &c., volunteered to go to the field of carnage. In one or two instances, preachers of the Brethren Church

volunteered, and actually went. One of them fell in the field of battle. In view of this state of things, it may well be imagined, that this year was not replete with the out-pourings of the Holy Ghost. There were some few revivals in the Church; but comparatively, they were few, and not very extensive. The spirit of war, and the weekly news from the scenes of deadly strife appeared to absorb all other interests. —William Hanby, *History of the church of the United Brethren in Christ (Part Second, 1825-1850, bound with Henry G. Spayth, History of the Church of the United Brethren in Christ).* Circleville, OH: Conference Office of the United Brethren in Christ, 1851, 316&317.

Philip Gatch and his family were traveling west when they came to the site of an earlier battle between the settler population and Indians in that area. That memory caused this reflection on war, peace, and holiness:

> …we arrived at Pt. Pleasant, on the Ohio. Here a great battle was once fought by our people and the Indians. What desolation war makes in the earth! Whence comes wars and fightings among us? St. James tells us, and also that there is nothing got by them. … The Scripture exhorts us to follow after peace and holiness with all men, without which we can not see the Lord. —John McLean, ed., *Sketch of Rev. Philip Gatch.* Cincinnati: Swormstedt & Poe, 1854, 97&98.

Charles Giles reflected much on war as an unchristian distraction, and about God's work of holiness in our lives as the remedy for all such distractions. At one point he was in Annual Conference, "on the Canadian shore, where we were kindly received, and hospitably entertained." He wrote,

> True religion is the offspring of Heaven, everywhere the same, always producing friendship and benevolence wherever it exists. If all mankind were truly converted and born of the Spirit, there would be no enemies in the world: all nations would form but one great family of brethren. Sin is the fruitful source of wars and animosities. Holiness, which is true Christianity, produces kindness, love, and harmony., - who then is truly happy? The Christian. —Charles Giles, *Pioneer.* New-York: G. Lane & P.P. Sandford, 1844, 246.

A major distraction in that century was growing affluence. While there were hard times for many, and periods of economic decline for society in general, industrious and hopeful populations across the continent saw growing enterprises and more prosperous communities. Benjamin Titus Roberts and the early Free Methodists saw this pattern as eroding the faith, values, and practices of Methodism. Affluence and social respectability were replacing simplicity and ministry with the poor by their parent denomination, the Methodist Episcopal Church. Large, impressive churches symbolized Methodist success, at the cost of pew rents and replacement of simple, utilitarian structures. Themes of evangelism and holiness and their attendant practices, camp and class meetings, declined as church members sought acceptance in surrounding society. B.T. Roberts wrote: "unmistakable indications show that prosperity is producing upon us, as a denomination, the same intoxicating effect that it too often does upon individuals and societies." Changes in the Methodist Episcopal Discipline "requiring that all our houses of worship should be built plain, and with free seats," and related changes "respecting dress, show that there are already too many among us who would take down the barriers that have hitherto separated us from the world. The fact that the removal is gradual, so as not to excite too much attention and commotion, renders it none the less alarming." — Benjamin Titus Roberts, *"New School Methodism,"* in Wilson T. Hogue, *History of the Free Methodist Church of North America.* Chicago: Free Methodist Publishing House, 1915, I: 101. Cf. Kevin M. Watson, *Old or New School Methodism? The Fragmentation of a Theological Tradition.* New York: Oxford University Press, 2019, and Howard A. Snyder, *Populist Saints: B.T. and Ellen Roberts and the First Free Methodists.* Grand Rapids & Cambridge, UK: William B. Eerdmans, 2006.

In Canada, a parallel history brought several Methodist groups together in a merged denomination that some saw as quite different from its origins. Free Methodists offered an alternative that worked for a deliberate return to older ways. —John Wilkins Sigsworth, *The Battle Was the Lord's: A History of the Free Methodist church in Canada.* Oshawa: Sage Publishers, 1960, 16-18.

But concerns along these lines also came from many who continued within the Methodist Episcopal Church, especially from those who had seen the changes happening over their lifetimes. Dealing with the problem of affluence, Charles Giles wrote,

> It seems to require more labour to bring some sinners to repentance than others. Some are encumbered and buried more deeply in the world than their neighbors; hence to arouse them, and bring them up into light and liberty, is a difficult task. ... The true worshippers of the holy God arise, as in primitive days, from the middle and lower classes.
>
> To be rich is a common desire among mankind, while poverty is universally dreaded. The notion seems to prevail that happiness always dwells with affluence, and misery with poverty. But this conclusion is formed merely from exterior appearances, and not from truth and philosophy. Great wealth brings burdensome care; and, moreover, places a man in imminent danger: powerful temptations surround his envied position. As a natural consequence, his soul's salvation is neglected, and his moral character sac-

rificed on Mammon's sordid altar. —Charles Giles, *Pioneer.* New-York: G. Lane & P.P. Sandford, 1844, 149&150)

James Finley was concerned with what he called "the almost universal spirit of speculation" or "money mania" which "seemed to have seized, like an epidemic, the entire people." This was a peculiar movement of "banking establishments" dealing with their own paper currencies. Finley also wrote about "the laying out of new towns," which was happening in his own Ohio and elsewhere:

> So great was the excitement, that towns were laid out at almost every cross road within a mile of each other, and on the tops of barren hills. It was no matter where they were located, plots were made, advertisements were stuck up, lots were sold, and magnificent squares left for public buildings. After this rage subsided, it is not to be wondered at that society was left in a deplorable condition. The imaginary riches of the speculator flew away like the morning cloud, and from a state of high excitement the community relapsed into a state of stagnation. —W.P. Strickland, ed., *Autobiography of James B. Finley.* Cincinnati: Methodist Book Concern, 1855, 273&274.

Jacob Young provided examples of speculation in wartime, which "gave the wealthy an opportunity to take advantage of the poor...." Sadly, the examples he gave were of Methodist local preachers. Thankfully, he balanced these with better behavior on the part of others. —Jacob Young, *Autobiography of a Pioneer.* Cincinnati: Cranston & Curts; New York: Hunt & Eaton, n.d., 309&310.

John Collins, like many of the older circuit preachers, watched his church change with the times, not always for the better. Growing affluence and related cultural changes were at the center of this concern. "Mr. Collins preferred the early forms of Methodism.... And it will be found, that wherever there shall be a departure from the primitive modes of Methodism, there will be a decline in the spirituality of the Church and in its growth." Included in his observations were the loss of simplicity in dress with the adoption of popular fashion, moderation in sermons and prayers in worship, and an increase in social and cultural respectability.

> Some individuals, proud of their acquired knowledge, and of their positions in society, may congratulate themselves on this advance of the Methodist Church. It is becoming more refined, and endeavors to accommodate itself to the improved taste and comforts of its members. And this, it is supposed, may increase the respectability of the Church. ,,, "for the world will love its own." The world hated the Author of our holy religion, and it can never love his disciples. The old paths have proved to be good, and they should be inquired after. By steadily walking in them, the Methodist Church has flourished, and has been the instrument of incalculable ben-

efit to the world. Let it not, then, depart from them, but rather suffer, that good may be done. —*A Sketch of the Life of Rev. John Collins.* Cincinnati: Swormstedt and Power, 1850, 117-120.

Alongside the distractions of war, nationalism, and prosperity was a strong opposition, shared by other Protestants, to the growing presence of Roman Catholicism in America. Some Methodist preachers in the States and in Canada had emigrated from Ireland, bringing inherited animosities with them. Converts from Catholicism in Quebec displayed intense criticism of their former church, as well as enthusiasm for their new denomination. While it was possible, with some difficulty, for many Protestant churches to unite in a common vision for their society, it was impossible for Protestants and Catholics to see a basis for cooperation in their common Christianity. Methodist preachers delighted in seeing Catholics liberated from their religious past and brought into the light of evangelical truth. Charles Elliott, a prolific writer against "Romanism," wrote a two-volume analysis of Catholic beliefs and practices. He believed "that Roman Catholicism is corrupt in its doctrines, morals, institutions, and practice, as a whole," yet he did admit,

> ...there is a *remnant* of truly pious persons among both the clergy and laity who have not defiled their robes. The pious few, whether lay on clerical, are guided by the remains of truth buried in their system, and the portions of it which are forced on them through the influence of Protestantism. By these means, the effect of error and of bad example is counteracted. These persons are good Christians, not in *consequence* of popery, but in *spite* of it. —Charles Elliott, *Delineation of Roman Catholicism.* New-York: G. Lane & P.P. Sandford, 1842, 8. Cf. Amand Parent, *The Life of Rev. Amand Parent.* Toronto: William Briggs; Montreal: C.W. Coates; Halifax: S.F. Huestis, 1887; D. Gregory Van Dussen, *"An American Response to Irish Catholic Immigration: The Methodist Quarterly Review, 1830-1870," Methodist History.* XXIX:1 (October, 1990), 21-36, and *"American Methodism's Christian Advocate and Irish Catholic Immigration, 1830-1870,"* Eire-Ireland. XXVI:4, 76-99.

The aggressive expansion of Methodism and the massive immigration of Catholics from Ireland and other countries brought a clash of cultures, histories, doctrines, and authority that could rarely see opportunity or desirability for the kind of mutual understanding and bridge-building that would come later in our history. John Wesley demonstrated the beginnings of that ability in his own writing. Methodists, Roman Catholics, and many other churches have changed a great deal in recent decades. Today we are free to envision *together* "the road to eternal life" on which Christians of many traditions are traveling. —Michael Casey, *The Road to Eternal*

Life: Reflections on the Prologue of Benedict's Rule. Collegeville, MN: Liturgical Press; D. Gregory Van Dussen, *Transfiguration and Hope: A Conversation across Time and Space.* Eugene, OR: Wipf and Stock, 2018.

Once distractions become habits, they can bypass critical thinking and dominate our lives in a way that can divert us indefinitely from our actual purpose, an observation as true for churches as it is for individuals. Habitual distractions must be replaced by healthy, fully Christian habits, capable of withstanding the world's distractions.

Chapter 6

Vision

"...we shall be like him, for we shall see him as he is." *John 3:2, NIV*

"Heaven already is begun...." Charles Wesley, "Let Us Plead for Faith Alone," *The United Methodist Hymnal*. Nashville: The United Methodist Publishing House, 1989, #385, v.3.

The idea of the road to glory has a very long history in Christian thought. One of its clearest expressions can be found in the sermons of the Irish monastic evangelist Columbanus (c. 543-615). Columbanus invited people to see themselves as "travelers and pilgrims in this world," with our true home in heaven, and this life as the road to that home. He saw that once we lose sight of our destination, the road itself – which is really "a fleeting and empty mirage," becomes, or takes the place of, our real home. "And so, since we are travelers and pilgrims in this world, let us think upon the end of the road, that is of our life, for the end of our way is our home." But sadly, "Many lose their true home because they have greater love for the road...." Therefore, "Let us not love the road rather than our home, in case we should lose our eternal home." We have to keep our destination clearly before us, "For a road is to be walked on and not lived in, so that they who walk upon it may dwell finally in the land that is their home." Thus, "we should live as travelers and pilgrims on the road, as guests of the world, free of lusts and earthly desires...." In this way, "we may joyfully and with a good conscience pass over from the road of this world to the blessed and eternal home of our eternal Father...." Our suitability for this ultimate home rests on the "great honor that God bestowed on men and women the image of his eternity and likeness to his own character." The road in this life is meant to prepare us for, and be consistent with, that character, which is the character of heaven itself. —Columbanus, in Oliver Davies &

Thomas O'Loughlin, eds. *Celtic Spirituality.* New York & Mahwah, NJ: Paulist, 1999, 353, 354 & 356.

When circuit riders envisioned heaven, it was in contrast to the harsher or mixed realities of this life. For Canadian preacher Alexander Byrne, "The path to heaven, though plain and well defined, is strewed with many sorrows and difficulties. ... These evils shall be redressed in the realms of bliss. Our powers shall be capacitated for our employment; and sickness, opposition, and sorrow, shall not impede our progress, or disappoint our hopes." One of Byrne's sermon outlines focuses on I John 3:2&3, as he reflects on "The Glorious Prospects of the Sons of God." In that sermon he is able to "disregard the things of earth" as he imagines what it will be like to "see him [Jesus] as he is," and to be "like him." The road to glory could be hard, but its end justified every hardship. —Sermons, in John Carroll, *The Stripling Preacher.* Toronto: Anson Green, 1852, 101; 179.

Daniel Wise described "the path of life" with the traditional expression "vale of tears." For him the contrast was clear: "Sorrow is the inalienable heritage of human nature. Grace may open a well of life in the converted heart; but the fountain of grief will be there also. Paradoxical as it may seem, a Christian is both 'a man of sorrows,' and a man of rare enjoyment." Thus, although Jesus warned his disciples, "In this world you will have trouble," he also spoke of the peace they would have, because "I have overcome the world (John 16:33, NIV)." Wise quotes a verse that promises: "The path of sorrow, and that path alone, Leads to the land where sorrow is unknown." —Daniel Wise, *The Path of Life.* New York: Carlton & Porter, 1847, 104.

In trying to give young people some understanding of life in heaven, Wise first said what heaven is not:

> In the heavenly life every cause of painful feeling will be absent. Read the beautiful statement of the Spirit respecting saved souls: *"God shall wipe away all tears from their eyes; and there shall be no more death, neither sorrow not crying, neither shall there be any more pain." No more pain, either of mind or body, to all eternity!* What a stupendous consolation!

Then he undertook the impossible but irreplaceable task of picturing at least some of what life in heaven will be like. In both cases, his images are taken directly, or by clear inference, from Scripture.

> On the other hand there is to be fullness of joy for evermore. God and the Lamb will anticipate and satisfy every want of their nature. Every intellectual aspiration will be gratified in the study of God's infinite being and productions, for we "shall SEE HIM AS HE IS." Every desire of the affections shall be met with delightful response, for to them shall be unfolded

the meaning of that unfathomed truth, "GOD IS LOVE." Every shape of perfect beauty shall charm the eye, and every sound of richest melody shall delight the ear. Read the gorgeous imagery by which the Revelator vainly sought to convey his impressions of the perfect purity and perfect bliss which he beheld in his inspired visions. Having read it, then consider his authoritative assertion: "IT DOTH NOT YET APPEAR WHAT WE SHALL BE!" After all God has revealed of heaven, the heights of its joys have never been scaled, the depths of its delights have never been fathomed. Eye hath not seen it; ear hath not heard it; nor hath human mind conceived it. It must be enjoyed to be understood. —Daniel Wise, *Pleasant Pathways*. New York: Carlton & Porter, 1859, 167&168.

Benjamin Lakin once wrote a sermon on "The Christian's Hope," part of which visualized the change we can look forward to in the nature of our bodies, based on Paul's words in I Corinthians 15, where he said, "So will it be with the resurrection of the dead. The body that is sown is perishable, it is raised imperishable; it is sown in dishonor, it is raised in glory; it is sown in weakness, it is raised in power; it is sown a natural body, it is raised a spiritual body." (I Corinthians 15:42-44, NIV) Lakin wrote, "The Christian is in hope that, when Jesus appears, we shall be like him in his glorified body. ... How far doth this exceed the glories of this world!"

Bishop Thomas A. Morris expressed this same thought: "Finally, the Christian hopes, that after the reunion of his soul and body, he will be glorified with Christ in heaven." Given this hopeful vision, "Why then linger with such a strange fondness on the shore of time? Our final home is over Jordan, and many of our best friends are there, waiting our arrival. Above all, Jesus is there, and, in due time, will come to pilot us over." Morris said this with no disregard for life on this side of that "river." He took both life and death very seriously, as Christians must. But he had seen people come to a point where holding on was both futile and painful, while moving forward in transition would bring peace and joy without measure. —Benjamin Lakin, "The Christian's Hope," *in Sermons on Miscellaneous Subjects.* Cincinnati: L. Swormstedt & A. Poe, 1859, 362; Thomas A. Morris, *"The Christian's Duty, Hope, and Privilege,"* in the same collection, 66&68.

In a similar way, Nathan Emery, stretching, as we all must do, to put this into words, spoke of a "heavenly rest" that would exclude the unhappy things in life, while placing us a better home.

> ...O, that 'sweet home,' that *heavenly rest*, which God has prepared for his people! What shall I say of it? Language fails in description – human intellect cannot grasp it. Imagination soars on trembling wing, only to be lost in its glories. Divine inspiration has given us a glimpse of it, by us-

ing the most grand and lofty figures of which our language is capable. ... [All of these and others tell us that] None of the feebleness of infancy, nor trembling of old age will ever be seen there. Sickly forms and funeral processions will never walk this golden pavement. It inhabitants bloom with perpetual youth. —Nathan Emery, "Christ the Christian's Savior and Redeemer," in *Sermons on Miscellaneous Subjects*. Cincinnati: L. Swormstedt & A. Poe, 1859, 200&201.

H.M. Eaton showed the role this vision of heaven played in the often sacrificially difficult lives of preachers' wives. These heroic women repeatedly left one home and circle of friends for another, "cut loose from worldly entanglements, ... afloat on life's troubled waters." Itinerancy demonstrated the hard reality that in this world we have no permanent home. "Along the way, however, the preacher's wife often knew enriching, encouraging fellowship," fellowship that would find its ultimate fulfillment in the life to come. As she looks ahead, she sees the perfect home she has been denied all her life, filled with those with whom she has shared "the path of life." (Psalm 16:11, NIV) In the "'furnace of affliction her heart was refined by grace, and she was fitted for the society of the blessed above.'" —H.M. Eaton, *The Itinerant's Wife*. New-York: Lane & Scott, 1851. 93&94; D. Gregory Van Dussen, *Circuit Rider Devotions*. Lexington: Emeth Press, 2019, 362&363.

As an older man, expecting the end of his life in this world, James P. Horton shared his vision of what was to come, in these words:

> Bless the Lord, I have not a doubt in my mind, but by his grace I shall reach the fair climes of ineffable beauty, and see my Father's children gathered from the four corners of the globe, and with them shine to the praise of his glory to all eternity, and gaze with rapturous love upon the beauty of Him that sitteth upon the throne for ever and ever. I expect the greatest wonder that will be there, will be that such a great sinner as I have been washed and made clean through the blood of the Lamb, and presented before the throne as a trophy of grace. But such is the good pleasure of my heavenly Father, for Jesus hath loved me, and given himself for me. Hallelujah for ever and ever! —James P. Horton, *A Narrative of the Early Life, Remarkable Conversion, and Spiritual Labours of James P. Horton*. n.c.: Printed for the Author, 1839, 205.

While there is a contrast between life as we know it here and life in the world to come, there is also continuity. The heart of the Wesleyan gospel was and is holiness, Christian perfection, sanctification – a growth toward God and our own destiny made possible by grace, the power of God to produce change in us. The purpose of Christian life is to grow more and more in the likeness of Christ, for in traveling this road the Spirit prepares us for eternity with God. There is no hope in looking forward to a transfer from one world to another without inner transformation. That kind of heaven would make our sinful state permanent, so that heaven would be a gathering place for all the evil we have known in this life. Instead, we ask God, in the words of the old Christmas carol, to "fit us for heaven to live with thee there." Fitness for heaven requires radical change – "perfection," Wesley called it - through God's power, so that instead of remaining forever as we are when we start the journey, we "are being transformed into his [Christ's] image with ever-increasing glory, which comes from the Lord, who is the Spirit (II Corinthians 3:18, NIV)." — *"Away in a Manger," The United Methodist Hymnal,* Nashville: The United Methodist Publishing House, #217, v. 3).

Since the road we travel, and the promised end of that road, are so completely connected, "Man's present and future destination do not at all differ in *nature*. In securing the true interests of this life, in right use and enjoyment of its blessings, we are making the best preparation for happiness in the life to come." Holiness brings happiness in this life and makes us ready for the life to come. Because holiness is God's character, for us to have eternal fellowship with God and to fulfill his purposes for our lives – he always seeks the best for us and in us – we must come to share that character, now and forever. "Future blessedness is but the continuation and perfection of that which commences here.... —"Nature, Condition, and Destination of Man," Sermon by Homer Clarke in Davis D. Clarke, ed., *The Methodist Episcopal Pulpit.* New York: Lane & Scott, 1850, 55.

Jacob Young left us wonderful testimonies of God's glorious presence in his ministry. In one of these, he wrote, "I thought I was one of the happiest mortals that breathed vital air." In another: "I had some trials and conflicts; but, when viewed with reference to the goodness of God toward me, they were not worth mentioning." In yet another: "My labor was very hard; but God apportioned my strength according to my day. I would become so amazingly blessed that I would want to take wings and fly away to heaven (Jacob Young, *Autobiography of a Pioneer.* Cincinnati: Cranston & Curts; New York: Hunt & Eaton, n.d.)." Likewise, Peter Cartwright said of his own experience on western circuits and districts, "I was much happier than many of the kings of the earth." —W.P. Strickland, *ed., Autobiography of Peter Cartwright.* New York: Phillips & Hunt; Cincinnati: Walden & Stowe, 1856, 302.

Young also saw the happiness of ministry in this life as circumscribed by old age. Yet he could face that limitation knowing that there was more goodness coming. Reflecting on his long ministry, Jacob Young wrote of the hope he had carried with him all his life. Thinking of colleagues who were "nearly all in eternity," he said, "How gloomy and melancholy is old age, unless rendered cheerful by the hope of a better life to come!" —Jacob Young, *Autobiography of a Pioneer.* Cincinnati, OH: L. Swormstedt & A. Poe, 1857, 271.

The heaven these early Methodists saw in the distance was also the heaven they experienced in worship. One early worshiper testified at a love feast, "...now I know heaven is not far off, but here, and there, and wherever Jesus manifests himself, is heaven." —Lester Ruth, *A Little Heaven Below: Worship at Early Methodist Quarterly Meetings.* Nashville: Kingswood, 240.

Many envisioned what heaven would look like, while others focused on the moral, spiritual, theological dimensions of participation in God's kingdom. W.H. Withrow pictured the early Canadian preacher Neville Trueman, gazing at a Niagara peninsula sky which, "transfigured and glorified in the light of the setting sun, seemed to the poetic imagination of the young man like the City of God descending out of heaven, with its streets of gold and foundations of precious stones...." —W.H. Withrow. *Neville Trueman, the Pioneer Preacher: A Tale of the War of 1812.* Toronto: William Briggs, 1900, 9.

In one of her sermons, Hannah Pearce Reeves compared heaven to Israel's long sought promised land. "She then expounded the text [Numbers 10:29] in reference to the celestial Canaan, and gave a glowing description of the joys of the heavenly world, and concluded with a pathetic appeal to the congregation, embellished with the most beautiful metaphors." — George Brown, *The Lady Preacher.* Philadelphia: Daughaday & Becker; Springfield, OH: Methodist Publishing House, 1870, 116.

Ezekiel Cooper saw heaven as continuous with our earthly pilgrimage. "How pleasant to travel in company with those who are also travelling to heaven." Such travelers move along life's highway together, in Christian fellowship.

Charles Giles wrote that their "sacred bond of unity extends from earth to heaven, connecting the children of God to God, their heavenly Father, and runs from heart to heart throughout the whole heavenly family." Here we see a deeply felt expression of the communion of saints.

Richard Allen looked ahead on that journey, to a time when "all our good old friends that are gone to Heaven before us, shall meet us as soon as we are landed upon the shore of eternity," accompanied by "the company of patriarchs, prophets, apostles and martyrs...."

Lester Ruth describes the journey of scattered Methodists to a Quarterly Meeting as "a concrete manifestation of a shared spiritual journey, the pilgrimage to heaven." —Lester Ruth, *A Little Heaven Below.* Nashville: Kingswood Books, 2000, 159; 152; Cf. Kenneth Barker, Gen. Ed. *Reflecting God Study Bible.* Grand Rapids, MI: Zondervan, 2000, p. 915, note on Psalm 121.

W.P. Strickland, reflecting on the death of Ralph Lotspiech, exclaimed, "How rich must heaven be in pure and sainted spirits, who have ... gone up to people its bright abodes!" —W. P. Strickland, ed., *Autobiography of Rev. James B. Finley.* Cincinnati: Methodist Book Concern, 1855, 237.

In a sermon called "The Present and Future State of Believers," Zechariah Paddock reminds us that God's people already have...

> ...an experiential knowledge of divine things. They have actually tasted of the good word of God and the powers of the world to come. God has given them ... "the earnest of the Spirit." Being united by a living faith to Him "who only hath immortality," they feel assured of an eternal residence with him in the kingdom of God. So much of heaven is already enjoyed by anticipation, nay, by actual *participation*, that to doubt its reality, would be to doubt their own experience, their own personal consciousness.

That participation might have taken place anywhere, at almost any time, but especially in worship, which became, like the ancient tabernacle, and then the temple, the meeting place between heaven and earth, where God dwelled in the midst of his people, in a temporary way that showed them what would one day become permanent. In worship, they experienced moments of profound bliss, glimpses of glory, in which all around them seemed transformed, with indescribable beauty. These glimpses created a longing for a time when there would be no return to the mixed reality of earth. Then,

> ...their bliss will be perfect. They will find the powers of their minds vastly enlarged, their faculties more vigorous, their imaginations more expanded, and, above all the principle of love more active. Introduced into this heavenly habitation, they will rejoice in a happy deliverance from their former frail and sorrowing tabernacle. And what a blissful change will this be to the saints of God! – a change from death to life, from affliction and distress to the most unmingled joys, from a sick and fainting body to a mansion of glory, from a state of corruption to a state the most holy and refined; in a word, from earth to heaven. —Zechariah Paddock, "The Present and Future State of Believers," in Davis W. Clark, ed., *The Methodist Episcopal Pulpit.* New-York: Lane & Scott, 1850, 167; 163.

In a similar way, D.D. Davisson envisioned, in a sermon called "The Christian's Legacy,"

> ...a perfect state of soul, gloriously enlightened, enlarged, ennobled, exalted – being made glorious in knowledge and wisdom, glorious in holiness,

inasmuch as it will be conformed to God, the being admitted into glorious society, even of the patriarchs and prophets, evangelists and apostles, saints and angels. This must also be a source of honor, and pleasure, and improvement – the having free, constant, uninterrupted communion with the Father of glory through the Lord of glory, and by the glorious Spirit.

"There we shall see, and hear, and know, All we desired or wished below; And every power find sweet employ in that eternal world of joy."
—W.P. Strickland, ed., *Rev. D.D. Davisson, Practical Sermons on Various Subjects.* Cincinnati: Methodist Book Concern, 1854, 227, including Isaac Watts, *"A Hymn for the Lord's Day" (v. 5),* www.Hymnary,org.

George White, in a funeral sermon for a friend, invited the congregation,

...let us all consider our ways, turn to the Lord, and strive to enter in at the strait gate, ...[that] we may have the same ravishing views of heaven, our departed sister had two days before her death, who said, she 'saw heaven opened, and heard the saints in glory sing: and like her, leave the world, crying, glory! glory! glory! even so, Lord Jesus. Amen! and Amen! — Graham Russell Hodges, ed.,, *Black Itinerants of the Gospel.* New York: Palgrave, 1993, 81.

Lorenzo Dow, following the vision of Adam Clarke, saw heaven as a place that would enlist and expand the soul. "In heaven ... no power of the soul, which is of utility here, will be diminished hereafter; but greatly strengthened and enlarged." In this way, each person will be "capacitated for the greater enjoyment in the realms above." —Lorenzo Dow, *History of Cosmopolite.* Wheeling: Joshua Martin, 1848, 507.

Adam Clarke had described the soul in heaven as "renewed in glory;" where gifts and talents given in this world,

...shall there have their consummation and plenitude of employ. Far be it from God to light up such tapers to burn only for a moment in the dark night of life, and then to extinguish them for ever in the damps of death. Heaven is the region where the spirits of just men made perfect live, thrive, and eternally expand their powers in the service and to the glory of Him from whom they have derived their being. —Adam Clarke, *Chirstian Theology.* Salem, OH: H.E. Schmul, 1967, 377-379.

In other words, that which had brought meaning, enjoyment, and purpose to this life would continue and expand in glory. There was no reason to lament what one left behind, for it would reappear and grow toward ever increasing perfection in eternity.

Human language has little choice but to use images from our experience in this world to at least point to realities in the next. We hope these images are helpful, though sometimes they may lead to confusion for someone who is overly literal. William Yost described a sermon he gave at a Pennsylvania camp meeting, including a question that stumped him:

> Preaching at the Mohontongo meeting, on the text, "Then shall the righteous shine as the sun in their Father's kingdom," [Matthew 13:43] I endeavored to illustrate that the Father's kingdom was the promised new Heaven and new earth in which dwelt righteousness, and was to be the eternal home of the people of God, after the purifying, conclusive processes of the last day. Father Bohner, in whose grove the meeting was being held, inquired whether, in that new and purified world, we would still have to contend with these surrounding high and rocky hills. The neighborhood was indeed a section composed of stony places. I could not answer the question. Who can? —William Yost, *Reminiscences.* Cleveland: Publishing House of the Evangelical Association, 1911, 113.

Nor did Methodist preachers neglect to share visions of hell, for heaven was neither automatic nor universal. The prevenient grace that enabled people to respond positively to God's invitation, also allowed them to turn aside and walk away. As John Wesley put it, "the refusing of a happy eternity implies the choosing of a miserable eternity. ... Therefore at the moment of death it [the soul] must be unspeakably happy or unspeakably miserable." —John Wesley, *"On Eternity,"* in Albert C. Outler, ed., *The Works of John Wesley.* Nashville: Abingdon, 1985, Vol. 2 (Sermons II), 367. So the invitation to eternal glory contrasted graphically with the threat of eternal damnation. Archibald McIlroy sometimes frightened his audiences with "scorching descriptions of hell," so that "It was no uncommon occurrence for his hearers, or at least some of them, to rush from the house in utter consternation." He used one illustration from Ireland to drive home the point to American congregations:

> I was once in Dublin when three hundred hogs were driven into town about sunset, and were butchered that night, and ready for market the next morning by sunrise. Where I lodged in my hotel, I could look out my window, and see the whole movement. The fire was burning, the smoke was rising, the water was boiling, the butchers were blaspheming and the hogs were squealing. I never ... saw anything in my life that so fairly and fully represents the damned in hell. —J.B. Wakeley, *The Heroes of Methodism.* Toronto: William Briggs, Montreal, C,W, Coates, & Halifax: S.F. Huestis, n.d., 350.

But the positive vision predominated, providing the hope needed for a victorious Christian life. Rooted in Scripture and the long history of Christian theology and spirituality, the Methodist vision took shape in the writings of the Wesleys and the early Methodist Bible Scholar Adam Clarke.

In this vision, heaven above was continuous with heaven below and was characterized by eternal, infinite growth. The road to glory was, for John Wesley, the life of sanctification leading to an eternity of blessing – "the way to heaven – how to land on that happy shore." At the end of that "way" is the new creation. Whatever else may be known about our destiny, "to crown all, there will be a deep, an intimate, an uninterrupted union with God; a constant communion with the Father and his Son Jesus Christ, through the Spirit; a continual enjoyment of the Three-One God, and of all the creatures in him!" For Charles it was transformation "from glory into glory, till in heaven we take our place, till we cast our crowns before thee, lost in wonder, love, and praise." —John Wesley, Preface to the Sermons, in Albert C. Outler, ed. *The Works of John Wesley.* Nashville: Abingdon, 1984, Volume 1: 105 and "The New Creation," also in Outler, Vol. 2, 510; Charles Wesley, "Love Divine, All Loves Excelling," *The United Methodist Hymnal,* Nashville: Abingdon, 1989, #384, v. 4; Albert C. Outler, ed., "The Way to the Kingdom," in Albert C. Outler, ed., *The Works of John Wesley.* Nashville: Abingdon, 1984, Vol. 1:231.

For Clarke, heaven is "The state of eternal glory," including "1. An absence of all suffering, pain, sin, and evil. 2. The presence of all good, both of the purest and most exalted kind. And 3. The complete satisfaction of all the desires of the soul, at all times, and through eternity...." Clarke wrote,

> Eternal life is the proper object of an immortal spirit's hope, the only sphere where the human intellect can rest, and be happy in the place and state where God is; where he is seen AS HE IS; and where he can be enjoyed without interruption in an eternal progression of knowledge and beatitude.

For Clarke, humanity's destiny is not so much an environment, though he does describe that, but God himself. It involves worship, especially singing, and the transfer from categories of time to those of eternity. It is the continued experience of transformation in unity with "brethren and holy souls." We will continue to fulfill our spiritual callings, and we will "make an eternal progression into the fullness of God," a "progression in unadulterated, unchangeable, and unlimited happiness." Hell is the opposite of all this. —Adam Clarke. *Christian Theology.* Salem, OH: H.E. Schmul, 1967, 378-380.

In a similar vein, D.D. Davisson preached about the Christian's destiny in heaven. In his sermon, "The Christian's Legacy," he said that heaven "implies a most perfect state of soul, gloriously enlightened, enlarged, ennobled, exalted – being made glorious in knowledge and wisdom, glorious in holiness, inasmuch as it will be conformed to God...." In "The Song of the Redeemed," a sermon reminiscent of Wesley's "The General Deliverance," Davisson speaks of freedom from all the evils and limitations of this life. Instead we will find "the grand scene of his glory" with "multitudes, as numerous as the drops of morning dew," as they "crowd into the realms of light, to ascribe 'glory, and praise, and honor to him that sitteth on the throne, and to the Lamb forever.'" In "The Christian's Portion," we are reunited in a kingdom that is "bright, beautiful, and blessed" with "our godly relatives and pious neighbors," along with "the worthies of other generations, patriarchs, and prophets, and apostles; martyrs, who ascended to the skies in chariots of fire, dropping their mantles, as they rose, of followers fit to wear them. We shall there be made pillars in the temple of our God, to go out no more forever." —W.P. Strickland, ed. *Practical Sermons on Various Subjects by Rev. D.D. Davisson.* Cincinnati: Methodist Book Concern, 1854, 10-12; 82&83; 52.

Zechariah Paddock said that "Benjamin Paddock [his brother] often assured people that God's loving provision would not end with death. In sermons, poetry, and conversations he offered hope beyond anything this world could give." One touching example is a poem he presented to his daughter as he gave her a Bible. In that poem he said,

> This is the gift I offer thee,
> True guide to an eternity
> Of life, of love, of rest.

Paddock took seriously Jesus' promise in John 14:2, concerning the place he would prepare for us in heaven, and he wanted his daughter and his fellow believers to live in that assurance. —Z. Paddock, *Memoir of Rev. Benjamin G. Paddock.* New York: Nelson & Phillips; Cincinnati: Hitchcock & Walden, 1875, 287.

Elbert Osborn had a light hearted, but accurate and powerful response to a question by the outspoken James Horton as they were on a steamboat, returning from a camp meeting. "Uncle Jimmy" Horton "was expressing, in a simple ye fluent manner, his hope of glory, and describing his expectations of meeting prophets, apostles, and martyrs, in the bright abode." He said to Osborne:

> "There," said he, "I expect, in the regions of the heavenly glory, to meet dear old father Wesley. And what shall I tell him from you, brother Osborn?" said he, turning suddenly to me. "Tell him that I am determined to meet him in heaven, and to get as many as I can to go there with me," was my answer. "I will," was the reply of the holy brother, and immediately he sat down. May God grant that this promise made to the sainted Wesley, through one who has since gone to join "the saints in light," together with all the solemn promises made to God by his unworthy servant, may be religiously kept. —Elbert Osborn, *Passages in the Life and Ministry of Elbert*

Osborn. New-York: Conference Office, 1847, 114&115.

Choctaw Methodist preacher John Page had a wonderful conversation with a little girl as he visited her family. Although her parents were not Christians, and she had not attended church or Sunday school, the visits Page or other preachers had made, taught her some of the basic truths of the Gospel, and she wanted to know more. Here is their conversation:

"Are you the heaven-talker?"
"Yes, said Page, "I am a preacher."
"Will you heaven-talk *now?*" "No, not now," said Page.
"Will you *heaven-talk* after we eat supper?"
"Yes, I will preach after supper. Do you love such *talk?*"
"Yes," said the child, "I do; for it will make our hearts good and then take us up to live with God in heaven."

Henry Benson commented on this conversation: "The child had learned the first lessons of Divine truth from the lips of the minister of the Gospel, and in listening to the word on two or three occasions only she had grasped the great and essential doctrines of practical religion." How sad that, in our time, these "great and essential doctrines" have sometimes taken second place to this-worldly concerns, and sometimes have dropped out of preaching altogether. Benson wrote that in the homes of these poor refugees, "there are many bright intellects that eagerly search for living truth and the messenger of Christ, with the Divine blessing, will gather many of them into the fold of the good Shepherd – jewels that shall bedeck the crown of the Savior." —Henry C. Benson, *Life Among the Choctaw Indians.* Cincinnati: L. Swormstedt & A. Poe, 1860, 189&190.

Like other circuit riders, John Page was a "heaven-talker." He made sure that heaven and the road to heaven were foremost in his teaching, so that even a young child got the point. The vision of eternity was so profound that it stretched the minds of Methodism's great theologians, yet could also be communicated to this little girl. For this we can praise the One who sent these preachers to carry and share this vision wherever they went. Since there are people in our own time who "eagerly search for living truth," the role of "the messenger of Christ" remains the same.

Chapter 7

Perspective

"Set your minds on things above, not on earthly things." —*Colossians 3:2, NIV*

"Till all the earth, renewed In righteousness divine, With all the hosts of God In one great chorus join, Join all on earth, rejoice and sing; Glory ascribe to glory's King" —Charles Wesley, *"God Is Gone up on High," Hymns of Faith and Life.* Winona Lake, IN: Light and Life Press; Marion, IN: Wesley Press, 1976, #184, v. 6.

Methodism has never fled from the world or left the world untouched by the Spirit who moved people along the road to glory. As Timothy and Julie Tennent put it, "The Christian faith is not some form of religious escape from the world. It is the faith that sustains us in the midst of real life, with all its challenges and trials." Only the most uninformed or hyper-critical would call the circuit riders' life an easy alternative to others they might have chosen. Christians have sometimes been accused of being so heavenly minded we're no earthly good. Nothing could be farther from the truth in the early period of our tradition, but the opposite might well be said of our movement today. (Timothy and July Tennent, *A Meditative Journey through the Psalms.* Franklin, TN: Seedbed, 2017, 92).)

    Evangelical pastor George Miller knew that salvation was a lifelong experience. Justification brought a radical and resolute turnabout, launching each Christian down a new road, with new purpose and energy. Sanctification meant that portions and regions of life were, both suddenly and systematically, brought into alignment with the character of God, and with his vision for his creatures. Glorification carried people through the transition to ultimate glory in the kingdom. Thus someone like Miller, who had served faithfully in ministry, could say at the point of death, "I know that I shall be saved." —R. Yeakel, *Jacob Albright and his Co-Laborers.* Cleveland: Publishing House of the Evangelical Association, 1883, 266.

The world view of these preachers was one of boundless hope. They sought continuous progress, not as something to be achieved by their own power, but by accessing the power of the Spirit. Through their ministry, God could accomplish anything, and when they had done all this life would allow, they died "in the full hope of eternal life." —John Dreisbach's description of John Walter, in R. Yeakel, *Jacob Albright and his Co-Laborers.* Cleveland: Publishing House of the Evangelical Association, 1883, 166&167.

In other words, their theology of, and life in, grace gave them a future orientation based on their trust, that in them and beyond them, God was building his new creation. Whenever strenuous efforts were required of them, they knew both the reason and the direction of that work. When insights from Scripture and dimensions of prayer took them farther into the depths of God and of life, they knew those depths were feeding their ongoing journey. Like Jesus himself, though in smaller measure, by the Spirit's power they could see, in themselves and others, oceans of possibility, forming a vision that could embrace all humanity in love and joy. When they saw people set free in the Lord, they rejoiced as if those people had been released from prison, for indeed they had. When they witnessed unlikely candidates go forth in ministry themselves, learning and growing as they went, developing into effective models and spokespersons for the kingdom, again they rejoiced in what God could do with ordinary human beings.

When the limits of this life had been reached, whether through age or sickness, violence or injury along the way, they experienced grief and pain, sorrow and loss. But they also saw the larger trajectory of grace that would carry the dying person through and beyond their Golgotha to their explosion into resurrection – their "eucatastrophe," as J.RR. Tolkien would later put it. They could look back in admiration at the road each person had traveled; the contributions made and the examples lived, but that was never the end of the story. —J.R.R. Tolkien, *Tree and Leaf.* London: George Allen & Unwin, 1975, 71.

There was no end, except for the chapter they had known in this life. This was not the terminus, but the transfer into "the kingdom of light." (Colossians 1:13, NIV) It was each person's micro-experience of the larger pattern that would result in a new and different time, beyond time, when "The kingdom of the world has become the kingdom of our Lord and of his Christ, and he will reign forever and ever." (Revelation 11:15, ESV) For those who were making that transition were "receiving a kingdom that cannot be shaken." (Hebrews 12:28, NIV) It was a kingdom, however, they had seen and entered when they were born again (John 3:3&5), one they had glimpsed in worship, in their own transformation, and in the transformation of others. They had seen God's glory, and now would live forever in that glory, heirs of the transfiguration of Christ that would, astonishingly, make them "like him." (I John 3:2, NIV) John Wesley had commented on I John 3:2 by saying that somehow they and we would experience "The glory of God penetrating our inmost substance." No wonder that the world could only scratch its head at these strange Methodists! "They know not what to make of us. We are a mystery to them." —John Wesley, *Explanatory Notes upon the New Testament.* London, Epworth, n.d., 910.

David Lewis knew - and this knowledge was shared by all of the preachers - that, along with other implications, to be converted was to begin the journey to everlasting life. We could say that revival preachers were travel agents for the road to glory. In his account of an Ohio camp meeting, he noted,

> Many were converted to God, became useful members of the Church, and still live to honor their profession; some of them holding official stations, are now standing in the fore front in the battle with sin and error. Some will read this sketch and say from the heart, "Thank God for that meeting! That was the time I started for heaven." God bless them! May they one and all obtain the crown of life! —David Lewis, *Recollections of a Superannuate.* Cincinnati: Methodist Book Concern, 1857, 293.

James P. Horton spoke hopefully about exchanging his worn out body for one that would never wear out:

> My spirit appears as young as ever, but I find my old tabernacle begins to fail. Now and then there is a pin dropping out, and then some of the siding gets loose, and so I am looking that it should fall before a great while. But, Glory to God! I have a better habitation reserved for me in heaven, that will never decay or get out of repair. —James P. Horton, *A Narrative of the Early Life, Remarkable Conversion, and Spiritual Labours of James P. Horton.* n.c.: Printed for the Author, 1839, 192.

Very often, preachers and others who were in the last days of their lives, would understandably focus their prayers and conversations on their expectation and even experience of final steps on their journey to heaven. A powerful example of this dynamic at work is found in the dying experience of William McKendree, one of the very early bishops of the Methodist Episcopal Church, shared with us by Bishop Joshua Soule. McKendree made a final pastoral tour, characterized by "patient suffering. Even though "it was obvious that he was gradually sinking to the repose of the tomb." Before long, "unable to perform the entire effective work of a General Superintendent of the Methodist Episcopal Church, his mind was frequently deeply exercised with the apprehensions that he might become unprofitable in the vineyard of his Lord." His and similar experiences among preachers demonstrated that they were in no hurry to leave their Christian involvement in this world. Their hope for eternity was not a death wish or a denial of life's importance. He served as long as he could before,

> He sunk patiently and sweetly into all his Heavenly Father's will, and waited in lively hope and abiding peace for the hour of its departure. The inward conflict had ceased; his confidence in God was unshaken; faith, strong and unwavering, stretched across the Jordan of death, and surveyed the heavenly country. With such sentiments, and in such a peaceful and happy frame of mind, the dying McKendree proclaimed in his last hours, "All is well!"

His last words were, "All is well for time or for eternity; I live by faith in the Son of God; for me to live is Christ, to die is gain." He died after an energetic ministry, not resigned to a terrible or meaningless fate, but surrendered to the One who would take him from there to the next stage of his God-centered, eternal life. —Joshua Soule, in Robert Paine, *Life and Times of William M'Kendree*. Nashville: Publishing House of the Methodist Episcopal Church, South, 1874, II: 173&274.

It is important to restate that the hope these preachers preached and lived did not emerge from or generate escapism or an unhealthy desire for martyrdom. They hoped to be ready when the time of their departure came, but they did not try to hurry that time. Focused on their ministry, they worked hard as long as they could. Inspired by visions of heaven, they were motivated to make a difference in this life, not by any premature desire to leave it behind. A good example is Jarena Lee, who after recovering from a time when her "health was much impaired," when she "knew not but that I should be the next one called away," resumed her ministry as soon as she was able. She believed that the "the Lord spared me for some other purpose, and upon my recovery I commenced travelling again, feeling it better to wear out than to rust out – and so expect to do until death ends the struggle, knowing, if I lose my life for Christ's sake, I shall find it again." —Jarena Lee, *in Spiritual Narratives*. New York & Oxford: Oxford University Press, 1988, 96&97.

Charles Giles had an inspired vision while still a child. After reading Bunyan's *Pilgrim's Progress*, he had a dream, one that stayed with him throughout his life. Its importance to the rest of us lies in its reflection of western Christian expectations about judgment and eternity. When combined with a natural fear of death, such a dream is a powerful motivator to take eternal questions seriously.

> ...I had a dream, in which the tremendous day of judgment was opened to my view. The dread tribunal appeared before me, and the Judge was seated upon his throne. A solemn crowd of human beings was gathered and gathering, and passing off to the right, or to the left, as the irrevocable sentence was passed. Not a word was spoken that reached my ear – a dreadful silence reigned. As I passed along toward the judgment seat, my mind was oppressed with anxiety and fears for myself and others in the crowd. After a momentary pause, without a word being spoken, I was permitted to turn to the right; thence I ascended, by an inclining passage, to a higher region. Instantly there opened on my wondering gaze an immeasurable field of delightful space: after casting a hasty glance over the scene, my attention was arrested by a sound of music advancing toward me, but at a great distance. The music was so unearthly, melodious, and inspiring, that I immediately became enraptured, and filled with sensations unutterable.
>
> In my joy and wonder I asked a heavenly being, who stood near me, what caused the melodious sounds which I heard. The being answered, "A company of angels singing." The tones increased in their thrilling power and sweetness as they drew nearer; but, before the seraphic band came in view, I was transported away in my dream to the lower world, and left among the common things of earth. After I awoke I found that it was a dream: still, the celestial melody seemed to sound on my raptured ear; and the deep impression which it made on my mind the changeful power of time has not wholly effaced. Though it was a dream, I was led to believe that there was a heavenly inspiration connected with it, from the effect it had upon my mind. —Charles Giles, *Pioneer.* New-York: G. Lane & P.P. Sandford, 1844, 29&30

Giles reflected further as he saw his own thoughts from an evangelical perspective:

> I was strongly impressed that the soul required a fitness for heaven which it did not possess by nature. Hence I often had fears, and a serious solicitude about my future happiness. The dying hour, the dark cold grave, and the judgment day, were subjects which often entered into my deliberations. If I laboured to divest my thoughts of such gloomy subjects, still, when any alarming event occurred, they rolled back again upon my troubled mind.

Later, in the midst of his experience of conversion, Giles had a vision that seemed to build on the one from his childhood, wiping away his doubts and fears:

> While I was there knelt before the Lord, with the eye of my mind directed

> heaven ward, a strait gate appeared to my view, which, it seemed, I had entered; and directly before me a beautiful narrow way opened, ascending to the throne of God. And on each side of this celestial highway I descried a dreary desert, where I saw many of my wretched fellow-beings wandering in darkness, entangled with spell and snares, groping their way amidst the dismal chaos. While gazing with wonder on the scene around me, I thought that I saw the glorious Angel of the covenant descending on this heavenly road, and, as he came near, part of his crimson mantle seemed to wave over me, impressing my mind, at the same time, with this solemn charge, "*Doubt no more!*" —Charles Giles, *Pioneer.* New-York: G. Lane & P.P. Sandford, 1844, 52&53; 72&73.

Visions and Dreams, together with and confirming Scripture and theology, all contributed to an expectation of something more after this life is over. Tragedy and death gave an urgency to these considerations. The idea that each life has an eternal, God-given purpose, and that each person is treasured by God, rendered the finality of death unacceptable, and the grave hideous.

But the promises of Scripture, clothed in familiar cultural expression, fed the hope that the grave is *not* our final destination, but part of a transition from one life to the next. Giles' vision included the distractions that hindered people along the way, as they were "entangled" and "groping their way amidst the dismal chaos" of life.

It often fell to the preacher to portray the reality of heaven, based on teachings and visions in the Bible, so that people could visualize it themselves. Nothing could match the actual experiences of heaven in worship, but there was also the need to push back the curtains and show the fullest panorama of Scriptural vision. One who could do this, in fact could portray nearly any Biblical scenario in ways that carried his listeners to the scenes he described, was John Newland Maffit. A.H. Redford wrote of Maffitt's preaching, "...we have never met with one who exercised such power over an audience as he did." Redford gives an extended picture of Maffit's preaching, including this portion on the way he elucidated the glorious vistas of heaven:

> We have listened to him as he spoke of heaven and portrayed its joys, until the jeweled gates rolled back, and walls of jasper and streets of burnished gold met our vision, and an innumerable multitude, with palms and crowns, were reposing beneath the boughs of the tree of life, or wandering along the banks of the beautiful river that makes glad the city of God; and we seemed to hear their songs of victory and shouts of triumph. As they exclaimed: "Unto him that loved us, and washed us from our sins in his own blood, and hath made us kings and priests unto God and his Father; to him be glory and dominion forever and ever." —A. H. Redford, *Western*

Cavaliers. Nashville: Southern Methodist Publishing House, 1876, 187.

This eternal perspective allowed people to see every part of life from a vantage point high above the confusion and discouragement they knew. This vantage point was a gift from God that included the wisdom to distinguish the worthwhile from the worthless in life. It helped them make key decisions, choose among relationships, and prioritize their lives and ministries around eternal values and hopes. Always the two roads lay ahead, with their opposite destinies, and each step led one way or the other. Perspective was different from the vision *of* heaven itself: it was essentially vision *from* heaven that clarified every part of this life and kept them on track to arrive at their destination. In especially vivid experiences, often during worship, they could see people and creation bathed in the light of heaven, surrounded by God's love and showing them what life should and would be like in God's kingdom. In the words of Orthodox theologian Alexander Schmemann "everything in Christ is able to participate in the eternal present of God." —Alexander Schmemann, *For the Life of the World*. n.c.: St. Vladimir's Seminary Press, 1973, 62.

An excellent example is the camp meeting experience of Mary Woods Apess:

> One day upon the camp ground, there was light from heaven shone into my soul, above the brightness of the sun. I lost sight of all earthly things – heaven was open to my view, and the glory of the upper world beamed upon my soul. My body of clay was all that hindered my flying up to meet Jesus in the air. How long I remained in this happy frame of mind I do not know. But when I came to my recollection, my Christian friends were around me singing the sweet songs of heaven; and I thought I was in the suburbs of glory. And when I saw them, they looked like angels, for they were praising God. I felt the love of God like a river flowing into my soul. From that time until the close of the meeting, I was happy. I now returned home rejoicing in God my Savior. —Mary Apess, in Barry O'Connell, ed., *William Apess, A Son of the Forest and Other Writings (1831)*. Amherst: University of Massachusetts Press, 1997, 82.

Bishop Richard Allen wrote of the role and extent of hope in his life, and the power of eternity on his road to glory:

> Who can contemplate the sufferings of God incarnate, and not raise his hope, and not put his trust in Him? What, though my body be crumbled into dust, and that dust blown over the face of the earth, yet I undoubtedly know my Redeemer lives, and shall raise me up at the last day; whether I am comforted or left desolate; whether I enjoy peace or am afflicted with temptations; whether I am healthful or sickly, succored or abandoned by the good things of this life, I will always hope in thee, O, my chiefest [sic]

infinite good. ...

Blessed hope! be thou my chief delight in life, and then I shall be steadfast and immovable, always abounding in the work of the Lord; be thou my comfort and support at the hour of death, and then I shall contentedly leave this world, as a captive that is released from his imprisonment. —Richard Allen, *The Life experience and Gospel Labors of the Rt. Rev. Richard Allen.* Nashville: Abingdon, 1960, 44&45.

CHAPTER 8

Companions

"Therefore encourage one another and build each other up, just as in fact you are doing." —*I Thessalonians 5:11, NIV*

"He bids us build each other up; and, gathered into one, to our high calling's glorious hope we hand in hand go on." —Charles Wesley, "All Praise to Our Redeeming Lord," *The United Methodist Hymnal.* Nashville: The United Methodist Publishing House, 1989, #554, v. 2.

In a letter to the Wyandott people, John Stewart called himself "your brother traveler to eternity...." That expression aptly describes the connection we have with each other as we walk the road to glory. Our conversations, activities, and experiences along the way are going somewhere. We share a common destiny, and that brings us together as one. Companionship is a wonderful, indispensable characteristic of our journey. On this road we teach and learn from each other, we share joys and sorrows, help lift each other's burdens, and lift each other up in prayer. Nothing we do together is insignificant, because it is part of the road God has called us to walk. Nothing we do is solitary, for together we worship and serve the One we call "Our Father." Children of this one God, we are brothers and sisters to each other: "...in Christ we, though many, form one body, and each member belongs to all the others." —*The Missionary Pioneer.* New-York: J.C. Totten, 1827, 55; Romans 12:5, NIV.

Circuit preachers and others involved in Wesleyan ministry found strength in the fellowship of their colleagues and the hospitality of circuits and local communities. James V. Watson describes what it felt like to experience hospitality on the circuit, which could provide an advance experience of our home in heaven:

With the feelings of a stranger, ...how cheering to the weary itinerant the hearty welcome with which he is wont to meet at a "household of faith!" In the bosom of that family, where the peculiarly fraternal spirit of Methodism reigns in all its ardor, its freshness, frankness, simplicity, confidence, and hospitality, he finds a balm for his disconsolation; a rest that relieves fatigue; goes far to reward his toils and compensate for his privations. Hospitality, always one of the richest graces of the hearth-stone, is sweetened into a feast of heaven when it flows in Christian sympathy and commingles with the communion of saints. How fruitfully suggestive in blessings to the self-sacrificing itinerant is the phrase, "a good home for Methodist preachers!" —James V. Watson, *Tales and Takings, Sketches and Incidents.* New-York: Carlton & Porter, 1856, 240.

When the preachers met for annual conference, and when they and other Methodist people cooperated in camp meetings, quarterly meetings, and other times of revival, they experienced a bond they could scarcely describe.

Commenting on preachers riding to Annual Conference, Jacob Young said, "You will rarely find, in any community, a happier set of men. We loved our God, our work, and one another." They traveled together and apart, and their earthly roads and pathways were signs of a greater pilgrimage. Charles Wesley pointed to this reality when he wrote, "We meet on earth for Thy dear sake, That we may meet in heaven." —Jacob Young, *Autobiography of a Pioneer.* Cincinnati: Cranston & Curts, New York: Hunt & Eaton, n.d., 201&202; Charles Wesley, *"Jesus, We Look to Thee," Hymns of Faith and Life.* Winona Lake, IN: Light and Life Press & Marion, IN: Wesley, 1976, #19, v. 3.

Nathan Bangs wrote of how hard it was for those attending Canada's first camp meeting, to leave each other and return to their separate lives and ministries.

> I will not attempt to describe the parting scene, for it was indescribable. The preachers, about to disperse to their distant and hard fields of labor, hung upon each other's necks weeping and yet rejoicing. Christians from remote settlements, who had here formed holy friendships which they expected to survive in heaven, parted probably to meet no more on earth, but in joyful hope of reunion above. The wept, prayed, sang, shouted aloud, and had at last to break away from one another as by force. As the hosts marched off in different directions the songs of victory rolled along the highways. Great was the good that followed. A general revival of religion spread around the circuits, especially that of the Bay of Quinte [in Upper Canada], on which this meeting was held. I returned to Augusta circuit and renewed my labors, somewhat worn, but full of faith and of the Holy Ghost. —Abel Stevens, *The Life and Times of Nathan Bangs, D.D.* New York: Carlton & Porter, 1863, 148&149. Portions of this quote appear

elsewhere in this study, but it deserves a place in this context as well.

A generation later, Toronto Methodists gathered a few miles outside of town for another camp meeting. John Carroll, who attended that event, spoke of the impact of such gatherings upon Christian fellowship:

> The effect of such meetings is to promote acquaintance and brotherly love between all the church, both ministers and members: and to check a tendency to secularism, and to promote heavenly-mindedness. The writer remembers the regret he felt at going back into the world after the meeting was over. Some of his most hallowed friendships were formed at that and similar meetings; friendships which have solaced him in this vale of tears from youth up to the present time, and friendships which he believes will be cemented and perpetuated. —John Carroll, *Past and Present.* Toronto: Alfred Dredge, 1860, 65.

African American Methodists had layers of difficulty to work through in order to enjoy the blessings of fellowship and mutual encouragement - barriers of race and class, slavery and its aftermath. Thus, for example, it was incumbent upon Bishop James Varick and subsequent leaders in the AME Zion Church to carry out "the great work of uplifting the race and of saving souls." Likewise Bishop Christopher Rush was known for "his love for Christ and the salvation of souls," and also care for the churches and "the wellbeing of his race." These layers of difficulty did not, however, eclipse their awareness that their pilgrimage in this life was headed somewhere else, and so we read that Bishop Rush "died in the full triumphs of faith," and Bishop J.J. Clinton's dying words were, "All is well, I am ready for the glorious change." —J.W. Hood, *One Hundred Years of the African Methodist Episcopal Zion Church.* New York: A.M.E. Zion Book Concern, 1895, 168; 171; 173.

An early American Methodist hymn connects the experience of worship here and in heaven, both involving us with other people. A portion of that hymn reads,

> In holy love let us begin
> This day our heaven below.
> Renounce the world, the flesh, and sin
> Lord, [give] life and light below.
> 'Tis heaven to meet our Jesus here,
> To praise redeeming love.
> Glory to God, we shall appear
> To praise in worlds above.
>
> With shining millions clothed in white,
> All prostrate at thy feet,

> In that blest world of love and light
> No more to part we meet. —Lester Ruth, *Early Methodist Life and Spirituality,* Nashville: Kingswood (Abingdon), 2005, 144&145.

Another is found in James P. Horton's autobiography:

> 'Tis there we'll reign, and shout, and sing,
> And make the upper arches ring,
> When all the saints get home.
>
> Come on, come on, my brethren dear,
> Soon we shall meet together there,
> For Jesus bids us come. —James P. Horton, *A Narrative of the Early Life, Remarkable Conversion, and Spiritual Labors of James P. Horton.* n.c.: Printed for the Author, 1839, 194.

Circuit riders payed tribute to their spouses as companions in ministry, though they tended to keep personal details about their marriages private. Those spouses who were still living were present during the time of the preacher's death and transition. They were the ones, along with other family members, who welcomed other pastors to visit and pray, and sometimes also to record the words and experiences of those final days. Spouses were among those who witnessed closing words of faith and visions of glory. The wife of Zechariah Ragan later wrote of this time, saying, "Had you seen your much loved friend in the last months of his life, as I did, you would have said, as did a visiting friend, 'There was less of earth than of heaven about him.'" —Ancel H. Bassett, *A Concise History of the Methodist Protestant Church.* Pittsburgh: James Robison & Baltimore: W.J.C. Dulaney, 1882, 486.

There is a continuity here between heaven below and heaven above, with a common thread of worship holding them together for these pilgrims, who were traveling the road together and would one day take part in the ultimate consummation of worship together. At that point their pilgrim band would join "shining millions clothed in white," never again, even for a moment, to lose the joy of intense fellowship.

In Canada, Bishop Walter Hawkins (British Methodist Episcopal) reached out in ministry to poor African Americans who had successfully made their way across the border. Committed as he was to unity among the Methodist family of churches, he also knew and responded to the special needs of those who, like him, had escaped slavery. He expressed gratitude to the General Conference of Canadian Methodism that "…you have received me like Christian gentlemen." But he also explained his special and separate mission of resourcing communities of former slaves and their descendants: "…I loved my dark brethren, and I went amongst them, and did what you cannot do – I unlocked the door of their hearts with a key which you could never get, and I sowed the seed there." He assured his fellow Methodists of the mainstream, white church in Canada, that theirs were separate organizations, "But we preach the same Gospel, we have the same ordinances; and I hope to live to see the day when we shall be one in name as we are one in faith." The BMEC remains a separate denomination to this day, yet Bishop Hawkins knew that even "if there never be a union here on earth, I expect to meet President Carman (of the Methodist Church in Canada) in heaven, here we will shake hands, and say, as we see all the members of our churches on the eternal shore: 'We helped to bring these to Jesus.'" Before he left that conference, the bishop introduced a song, saying, "…aren't we all going to the same heavenly home?" – and then sang,

> I'm nearer my home,
> I'm nearer my home,
> I'm nearer my home, to-day,
> I'm nearer my home, where Jesus has gone,
> I'm nearer my home to-day.

The response was a thunder of voices, united across the conference, led by its chairman.

> The venerable Dr. M'Mullen, the representative of the British conference, found himself singing and swaying with the rhythm; about five hundred voices, above and below, sang that chorus with a volume of energy and feeling that swept every tittle of the conventional clean out into the street.

Clearly the bishops and delegates at the conference felt and knew the unity that bound all Wesleyans together, even with their different denominations, and in that unity shared a common hope and assurance of eternal life. That common hope and assurance provided the great resource of companionship that could scale the walls of historical divisions.

Even the special circumstances of Bishop Hawkins' church pointed to their ultimate goal. The bishop sang, "On my way to Canada," and explained, "This is my earthly home. But it was heaven to me in the old days, and many a time this song cheered my heart for it seemed to anticipate heaven." Thus he sang, "I'm on my way to Canada, where the coloured man is free." Freedom in this world reflected eternal freedom in the next.
—S.J. Celestine Edwards, *From Slavery to a Bishopric.* London, UK: John Kensit, 1891, 159-162.

We tend to think of God and family and people with whom we share a common faith as our chief companions on our journey. Bishop Hawkins reminds us that fellow Methodists are such companions. What we may not often consider is that even now the host of heaven surrounds us with encouragement and support! When Paul spoke of his impending death, he likened it to finishing a race. (II Timothy 4:7&8) No race or other athletic competition is complete without cheering crowds of people who care about our finishing well. This is the "great cloud of witnesses" in the similar comparison given in Hebrews 12:1. Many of the Communion services in those days included the recognition that the gathered congregation was praying in that larger context: "Therefore with angels and archangels, and all the company of heaven, we laud and magnify thy glorious name...." Whenever Methodists, or other Christians, prayed together in common worship, they joined the worship already taking place in God's eternal kingdom. This we see expressed in one of Charles Wesley's hymns,

> Come, let us join our friends above who have obtained the prize, and on the eagle wings of love to joys celestial rise. Let saints on earth unite to sing with those to glory gone, for all the servants of our King in earth and heaven are one. —*The Doctrines and Discipline of the Methodist Episcopal Church.* New York: J. Emory and B. Waugh, 1828, 94; Charles Wesley, *"Come, Let us Join Our Friends Above," The United Methodist Hymnal.* Nashville: The United Methodist Publishing House, 1989, #709, v. 1.

In his sermon following the death of Rev. Seth Mattison, Israel Chamberlayne envisioned the scene as a Christian "runner" finished the race: "The heavens peal with the explosive shouts of the spectators. The palm he waves proclaims the victor. The triumphant wreath is his." All are gathered around the One who has brought them there. "And, above all, a near and intense gaze on the unveiled face of God incarnate, in whom all the Father's and the Spirit's glory will shine for ever." Clearly this "cloud of witnesses" is among the companions on the journey, and their companionship is a significant, though not always acknowledged, resource along the way. —Israel Chamberlayne, "The Past and the Future, as Surveyed by a Faithful Minister of Christ, at the Hour of Dissolution," in Davis W. Clark, ed., *The Methodist Episcopal Pulpit.* New York: Lane & Scott, 1850, 381.

CHAPTER 9

Resources

"May our Lord Jesus Christ himself and God our Father, who loved us and by his grace gave us eternal encouragement and good hope, encourage your hearts and strengthen you in every good deed and word." —*II Thessalonians 2:16&17, NIV*

"…by thine all sufficient merit, raise us to thy glorious throne." —Charles Wesley, "Come, Thou Long Expected Jesus," *The United Methodist Hymnal.* Nashville: The United Methodist Publishing House, 1989, #196, v. 2.

God himself was the chief companion and resource on this journey, feeding and encouraging preachers' hearts, equipping them with needed gifts, teaching them valuable lessons, and guiding them on their way. Preachers sought that same companionship for their people and churches. He spoke to them in many ways, especially through the words of Scripture. James O'Kelly, leader of the first (and short-lived) breakaway movement in American Methodism, wrote a hymn that asked God to unite the church, "And make thy word their guide to heaven." O'Kelly called the Bible "the lamp" that "marks my way to heaven." He envisioned at the end of his road "BRIGHT mansions of eternal love" beyond "the monster death." These "thoughts of bright glory" allowed him 'to view the blessed goal.…" Though death was to him "the king of terrors," it was also "The road to everlasting joy!" —James O' Kelly, *Hymns and Spiritual Songs.* London, UK: Forgotten Books, 2015, Hymns #62&65; Songs #9, 11 & 17.

In much the same way, Evangelicals sang that "death must yield to love." But experiences of heaven did not wait until after death. They testified to being "full of glory" even in this life. One of their hymns said,

The smiles of bright glory,
Appear on my soul;

> I sink in bright visions,
> I view the bright goal - *Evangelical Association of North America, A Collection of Hymns (etc.).* London, UK: Forgotten Books, 2015, #146, 147 & 152.

The goal, and the resources to arrive there, strengthened them and enabled them to strengthen others for the journey. (II Corinthians 1:3-7) For God, "our help in ages past," was and is "our hope for years to come." Even from the hope-deprived anguish of slavery, Charles Thompson could say,

> I was a slave, and was compelled to labor for the profit of my owner, which I performed diligently and faithfully; I was a child of God, and owed him duty and obedience, which I performed earnestly and constantly. From my slave-owners I expected and received no reward or remuneration; from God I received no pay as I labored, but my great reward is yet to come. I have been a depositor in God's bank, from which I expect to draw largely at the final settlement. —Isaac Watts, "O God! our Help in Ages Past," in *A Collection of Hymns, for the Use of the United Brethren in Christ.* Dayton: W.J. Shuey, 1871, #820, v. 1; Charles Thompson, *Biography of a Slave, Being the Experiences of Rev. Charles Thompson, a Preacher of The United Brethren Church.* New York, NY: Dossier Press, 2015, n.p.

Worship was a primary resource and motivator for preachers and congregations alike, whether it happened in homes, school houses, barns, or churches. In worship God met them, poured his Spirit upon them, and started and continued them on the path of life. This was especially true of quarterly meetings and camp meetings, which brought people together for extended worship, and class meetings, which were small and local, but could be more personal and sometimes more intense than other forms of worship. Sadly, quarterly meetings would give way to quarterly conferences, and eventually to charge conferences and congregational meetings (and their district counterparts), which had very different purposes. George Coles describes the contrast between old time quarterly meetings and quarterly conferences:

> The old-fashioned quarterly meeting was a real religious festival, and very profitable. A quarterly-meeting conference now held on some evening in the week, is a mere business meeting, without sermon, love-feast, or sacrament. [At one quarterly meeting] we met on Friday, and did not finally separate until Sabbath afternoon. We had four sermons, a prayer meeting, a love-feast, and the sacrament of the Lord's supper. —D.P. Kidder, ed., George Coles, *My First Seven Years in America.* New-York: Carlton & Phillips, 1852, 82.

Those resources we call the means of grace – Scripture, Sacraments, love feast, preaching, etc. - were powerfully present in the original quarterly meetings, and nearly absent from their successor events. People would make great sacrifices to attend quarterly meetings, sometimes traveling over dangerous roads in terrible weather. It is hard to imagine anyone sacrificing to attend a charge conference today, unless attending *is* itself the sacrifice in order to accomplish a church's practical needs. Few people expect to be inspired by such meetings, yet in those early days, inspiration was everywhere to be enjoyed.

David Lewis gives us an account of a quarterly meeting held in a barn, in winter, at the north end of Lake Champlain!

> "What, hold quarterly meeting in a barn, in the dead of winter?" Yes, reader, I have attended a number of such. On those occasions we had crowds of people, and no meeting-house. We would then resort to the barn, and, giving the floor to the women, the men would take the loft, sit close together, with hearts warmed with divine love, and sing, and pray, and shout the praise of God, with hearty good-will. —David Lewis, *Recollections of a Superannuate (etc.)*. Cincinnati: Methodist Book Concern, 1857, 68&69.

Samuel Howe describes one particular quarterly meeting, and the impact Jacob Gruber had on the gathered congregation when he prayed following another preacher's sermon.

> At a quarterly meeting held in a barn in this part of the country, after a most impressive and powerful sermon from the presiding elder, M'Lenahan, Gruber engaged in prayer. "It seemed, says Father Howe, "to resemble the day of Pentecost; the barn was shaken, and the people simultaneously sprang to their feet, while shouts of joy and cries for mercy filled the place. Many fell to the floor, and others were filled with fear and fled in the greatest consternation. —W.P. Strickland, *The Life of Jacob Gruber.* New York: Carlton & Porter, 1860, 24.

At a modern charge conference, there might well be people who leave in a state of "consternation," but it is unlikely to come from Pentecost breaking out! The role of these larger gatherings in providing spiritual resources for the road to glory is unmistakable in the testimonies of those who were there.

Valentine Cook testified to the wisdom and power of Scripture as a resource for his eternal pilgrimage. Not long before his death, Brother Cook preached at a camp meeting, taking for his text a passage that well expressed Christian destiny.

> As usual, he labored with great zeal and success. He preached on the Sabbath to a vast crowd, from these words: "For our light affliction, which is but for a moment, worketh for us a far more exceeding and eternal weight of glory." 2 Corinthians iv, 17. After a solemn and very impressive pause,

he lifted his eyes to heaven and said: "What! Our *afflictions* work for us a weight of glory! - a far more exceeding and eternal weight of glory!" and added: "I believe it with all my heart, because thou, O God, hast revealed it in the blessed volume."

Cook and his colleagues in those early generations of Methodist preachers, found the Bible to be formative in their perceptions of heaven and in charting the trajectory of their lives. Thus "he died as he had lived, 'strong in faith, giving glory to God.'" In a similar way, Robert Lusher encouraged "a scriptural hope of eternal life," hope that was always part of the road to glory, which aimed at "a full conformity to the image of God...." —George Peck, *Early Methodism within the Bounds of the Old Genesee Conference, (including words from Cook's biographer, Edward Stevenson).* New York: Carlton & Porter, 1860, 102&103; John Carroll, *Case, and His Cotemporaries.* Toronto: Wesleyan Conference Office, 1869, II:277.

L.D. Davis provided a very special resource for those dealing with an all too common reality in those early days, the death of a child. His book, *The Child in Heaven*, helped grieving family members through one of the saddest experiences in life, yet one that, for Christians, could be "the pathway that leads to life." —L.D. Davis, *The Child in Heaven.* Syracuse, NY: E.H. Babcock, 1853, 14.

Experienced preachers could serve as a great resource for younger ones, as Elijah Woolsey was for George Coles. This veteran of many circuits "could tell me all about the 'Lights and Shadows' of itinerancy. I therefore called upon him, and received from him such directions and advice as enabled me to prosecute my journey with great pleasure, and to reach the end of it in safety." —D.P. Kidder, ed., *George Coles, My First Seven Years in America.* New-York: Carlton & Phillips, 1852, 104&105.

Nor did the heavenly goal keep early Methodists, black, white, or indigenous, from seeking to improve life in this world. James Finley and John Stewart worked for years on behalf of the Wyandotte Indians of northeastern Ohio, while Peter Jones, John Sunday, and Peter Jacobs (and many others) worked tirelessly for native people in Canada. Charlotte Riley worked within the African Methodist Episcopal Church to better the lot of former slaves. Their activism was supported by their faith and the trajectory of their journey. Sister Riley testified to "a hope as 'bright as the promise of God' that we shall meet again in that world where death can never enter to part us any more, 'Glory Hallelujah, praise the Lord!'" — Crystal J. Lucky, ed. *A Mysterious Life and Calling: From Slavery to Ministry in South Carolina.* Madison: University of Wisconsin Press, 2016, 53.

It was said of Methodist scholar John McClintock, "If he had had a hundred hands he would have lent them all, in help and service, to his fellow-men. 'To look up and not down, and to lend a hand,' were the sum and substance of his philosophy of life.'" —George R. Crooks, *Life and Letters of the Rev. John McClintock.* New York: Nelson & Phillips; Cincinnati: Hitchcock & Walden, 1876, 317.

For all people in our tradition, "the preacher is a messenger of heaven," one who speaks out of intimate communion with the God of heaven and earth, who loves his people and provides truth and guidance so that we can travel safely and reliably home. Worship, such as that of the old time quarterly meetings, made the place of worship "the gate of heaven," where preachers and others broke through the boundaries between the kingdom of God and the ordinary realities of this world. The convert was "an heir of heaven," one who had been adopted by faith into God's family and who now would make the journey, with his new family, to that family's ultimate home. —Genesis 28:17, NIV; Charles Giles, *Pioneer.* New-York: G. Lane & P.P. Sandford, 1844, 86&88.

The poverty, hardships, and even persecution of circuit riders are not as surprising as their resilience and the resources that animated their lives and ministries. Methodist Episcopal Bishop Thomas A. Morris wrote,

> Those who look not beyond the things which perish, and take no thought for the life to come, might naturally suppose that the early Methodist preachers of this country, according to the preceding remarks respecting their difficulties, were very disconsolate men. And truly, in view of the things they suffered, there would be some plausibility in this supposition, if in this life only they had hope. But not so. They sought a better country, laying up a good foundation against the time to come; and their hope was anchored within the vail, whither Christ, the forerunner, was for them entered, as an advocate with the father. When a man glories not, save in the cross of Christ, by which he is crucified to the world and the world to him – when he has ... a good hope, through grace, of everlasting life in heaven, he will be happy under any outward circumstances. Now, this was the condition of most Methodist preachers.... There may have been exceptions; but the great body of them knew that their witness was in heaven, and their record on high, while they received within their hearts a kingdom which could not be shaken by the combined opposition of Satan and his children.

Morris goes on to mention "peace in believing, and joy in the Holy Ghost;" the blessings of "the sweet solitude of the woods, so favorable to pious meditation" for the army of preachers on the North American frontiers; the joy and fellowship of worship, even in the remotest of places, and the abundant fruits of their labor, for "the handful of members have swelled to multitudes, and the place of the log hut, in which we once met to worship, is supplied with a spacious chapel, and is still full. Truly, 'the Lord has done great things for us, whereof we are glad;' and the blessed work is still going on." —Thomas A. Morris, *Miscellany*. Cincinnati: L. Swormstedt & A. Poe, 1854, 259-263.

The resilience and ingenuity of those early preachers became proverbial. Most of this creativity was expended in bringing people to Christ and building the infrastructure of the church, but there are also stories – some of them hilarious – of circuit riders tackling certain practical difficulties in unexpected ways. Here is Thomas Morris trying to remedy an overabundance of flies at his Columbus, Ohio parsonage. It is important to remember that parsonages were uncommon at the time of this incident (1830), and their condition could be appalling. In this case, the pastor and family shared a two-room house with stables nearby.

> On the smooth surface of a broad board I poured a small stream of honey so as to form a circle; immediately adjoining which, I formed an outer circle of gunpowder, with a connecting arm extending at right angles six inches, so as to ignite without frightening the enemy. When the whole circle of powder was covered with flies, two or three deep, with their bills in the honey, I applied a red-hot rod to the connecting train, blowing up hundreds at a blast. A few such operations each day left us in the quiet and peaceable possession of the field. —John F. Marlay, *The Life of Rev. Thomas A. Morris*. Cincinnati: Hitchcock & Walden; New York: Nelson & Phillips, 1875.

Whatever resources supported pilgrims on the road to glory were ultimately expressions of grace, the transformative power of the Holy Spirit at work in believers' hearts and lives, producing holiness of spirit, character, lifestyle, and action, in ways and measures appropriate to every stage of the journey. Nathan Bangs said,

> ...that our salvation, from beginning to end, in its most incipient stage, through every step of its progress, from conviction of sin to pardon, and from that to full sanctification, and then onward in the way of holiness, until we arrive to the kingdom of eternal glory, is all of GRACE – the rich, abounding GRACE OF GOD IN JESUS CHRIST....

Nothing that is part of this pilgrimage is self-generated, or based in human will power. Even good practices, apart from grace, fall short of their divine purpose in us and in those whose lives we touch. Bangs continued:

> Neither reading nor hearing the word of God, partaking of the holy sacraments, repentance, prayer, nor even believing, will be effectual to this or any other degree of salvation, only so far as it may be accompanied by the

operation of the Holy Spirit upon the heart – in the inmost soul, moulding it into the image of God. —Nathan Bangs, *The Necessity, Nature, and Fruits of Sanctification.* New York: Lane & Scott, 185; 201.

Alexander Byrne spoke of "the means of grace appointed for your advancement in holiness." In doing so he described a full offering of resources for the road to glory, resources important for the journey and its destination, which in fact are inseparable:

> It is evidently the design of every sacred ordinance to make you meet for the saints in light. I admit that many, if not all these means, have a secondary use, with regard to the circumstances of your present state; but that you may attain the kingdom is the grand ultimate of all.

It is significant that such a mature statement came from one who lived only 18 years (1832-1851), yet was a much acclaimed preacher. Byrne's last words were "I know that my Redeemer liveth." Clearly one source of inspiration and endurance, even for such a young preacher, was the fact that he lived "in hope of his final reward." —John Carroll, *The Stripling Preacher or a Sketch of the Life and Character ... of the Rev. Alexander S. Byrne.* Toronto: Anson Green, 1855, 195, 57, 55, 177.

Another resource came in the form of manuals and guidebooks for revivals in general and camp meetings in particular as engines of transformation, and class meetings and Sunday Schools as conservators of transformation. As the churches matured in the development and use of these gatherings, they grew in their understanding and appreciation for them, shared best practices, and learned from mistakes. As time went on they had to answer criticisms and adapt to new circumstances.

Among the resources available for these purposes were B. W. Gorham's *Camp Meeting Manual,* which provided detailed information on setting up and operating a camp ground. This book, published in 1854, came more than fifty years after the first camp meeting at Cane Ridge, long enough for developing expertise, but also generating opposition. Gorham was himself a camp meeting preacher who knew that form of ministry intimately. He was led to produce his manual, in part, by the realization that, especially in his part of the country, New York State, some "Methodists, both preachers and people, were to a considerable extent, apparently disposed, silently and gradually, to abandon the use of Camp Meetings." He believed that camp meetings had by no means worn out their usefulness, but that they could be improved, "making the most of them for the practical ends they seek to accomplish." One of the reasons he believed such gatherings were so successful was: "They call God's people away from their worldly business and cares for several successive days, thereby securing time for the mind to disentangle itself of worldly care, and rise to an undistracted contemplation of divine realities." Among the many ways camp meetings served as means of grace, or clusters of means of grace, was their ability to combat distractions. Gorham believed that,

> ...with all the other usages of Methodism, there is still wanting some season of great and general religious interest, that shall convoke these men of God in considerable numbers, and permit them, disburthened of all worldly care, to drink together at the fountain of mercy, to cement their friendships at the foot of the cross, and to lose their selfishness, and pride, and unholy ambition, while bathing together in a common ocean of love.
> —B.W. Gorham, *Camp Meeting Manual*. Boston: H.V. Degen, 1854, vii&viii; 17; 37&38.

Other resources addressed the benefit of revivals generally, again against the backdrop of erosion of support in some quarters. James Porter, again in 1854, published his book on revivals, arguing as Gorham did for their necessity, and also for their improvement. Among their benefits is that "The tendencies of the mind are changed. Formerly they inclined to temporal things, now to spiritual; then to the earth, now to heaven." Porter believed that everything a church does should promote the purposes of revival. For example, in the Sunday School, "Teachers should make the conversion of their pupils their leading object. All their instructions ought to be of such a character, and so applied as to contribute to it." Every Christian should support this kind of Christian education. "Christians who neglect the Sabbath school, know not what they do, or they are criminally at fault." Sensing that the unified purpose of Methodist churches was fragmenting and losing steam, Porter urged pastors and leaders to push aside distractions and discouragement and reintegrate the church to its original focus. —James Porter, *Revivals of Religion*. New-York: Carlton & Phillips, 1854, 25; 37&38; 149.

Another example of this genre is Luther Lee's *Revival Manual* (1850), which argued forcefully against what Lee saw as the growing worldliness of the churches. He made this point abundantly clear in his preface:

> The writer believes that revivals are the life and the hope of the church, and that without them she would soon relapse into a state of dead formality, and become as destitute of the power of Godliness as those religious establishments, with whom membership depends upon birth-right and not a change of heart.

His book put forth both the "vindication of revivals, as well as useful suggestions in relation to the means of promoting them." Among the blessings of revivals, protracted meetings, and camp meetings, was significant change in the lives of participants who came for vague or extraneous reasons, but left with their faces set in a new direction.

> The process is simply this, sinners who are careless and prayerless, and are "without hope and without God in the world,' have their attention called to their spiritual interests, and see their guilt and danger; they feel a deep sense of guilt, and form a deliberate purpose to forsake sin, and to obey God in the future; they do actually reform their habits, they go to God in prayer, and asking for pardon through faith in Jesus Christ, they receive the remission of their sins, and "being justified by faith they have peace with God through our Lord Jesus Christ."

All such transformations result from the power of the Spirit present in times and places of revival. But even radical changes in behavior are only part of what revivals produce. Lee points out that revivals have been the turning point, the point of conversion, and the platform launching people into ministry and other forms of Christian leadership and service. He asks his readers to notice that "a very large portion of the present ministers of the gospel, and far the greatest number of the living, working Christians, were first brought to Christ during revival scenes." Thus to denigrate or abandon revivals is to undermine and disempower the Church. —Luther Lee, *The Revival Manual*. New York: Wesleyan Methodist Book Room, iv; 11&12; 54.

A resource available to married circuit riders and local preachers came from their spouses. In a few cases, such as Hannah and William Reeves, they were both ministers, assigned to circuits together, leading revivals together, and able to talk over the ups and downs of ministry together. —George Brown, *The Lady Preacher.* Philadelphia: Daughaday & Becker; Springfield, OH: Methodist Publishing House, 1870; Elizabeth Gillan Muir, *Petticoats in the Pulpit: The Story of Early Nineteenth-Century Methodist Women Preachers in Upper Canada.* Toronto: United Church Publishing House, 1991, 52-103.

For others, such John B. Hudson, the preacher's wife shared as much as she could the burdens of his ministry while raising their children.

> My wife doubtless felt the inconvenience of being left with five small children, among strangers; but it was then and always has been to me a source of consolation and encouragement, that she never was disposed to complain or fret; but, on the contrary, did all that was practicable to help me on in my trials and travels. I have often thought, had she been otherwise disposed, I should have sunk. But, thank God, she was ever with me in heart and hand, in relation to the Gospel. —John B. Hudson, *Narrative of the Christian Experience, Travels and Labors of John B. Hudson (etc.).* Rochester, NY: William Alling, 1838, 85. Cf. Marilyn Fardig Whiteley,

Canadian Methodist Women, 1766-1925 (etc.). Waterloo, ON: Wilfred Laurier Press, 2005, 37-59; H.M. Eaton, *The Itinerant's Wife (etc.).* New-York: Lane & Scott, 1851.

In still other cases, the preacher's wife accompanied her husband on his rounds and took an active part in his ministry. In 1811, Mrs. Loring Grant "rode extensively over the circuit with her husband, and often followed his sermons with an earnest and melting exhortation." George Peck reports that her speaking "was always well received by the people. —George Peck, *Early Methodism within the Bounds of the Old Genesee Conference.* New York: Carlton & Porter, 1860, 340; 346.

A further resource on the road to glory is the wealth of sermons and other books provided by the various Methodist publishers at that time. While the books that circulated, often carried in the circuit riders' saddlebags, certainly helped with the day to day spiritual and practical religious needs of people in this life, they also formed part of their consciousness and preparation for the life to come. Especially important in this regard were sermons and biographies, excerpts of which appear throughout this book. These gave people both context and example with which to approach their own deaths and the deaths of others. They lifted people's eyes from a preoccupation with the details of everyday life and shined a light ahead on the path they were walking.

Manuals for preachers, from Wesley's delineation of pastoral character and responsibilities to Coke and Clarke's *Preacher's Manual*, to more elaborate catalogs later in the nineteenth century, provided a daunting array of expectations. Daniel Kidder's book gave what could well read like a withering list of duties and characteristics, but also included those parts of a pastor's life that are filled with grace and encouragement, culminating in God's eternal promise. One form of encouragement and joy comes when we see our work bearing fruit in the lives of those we have served. Kidder paraphrases II John v.4, for example: "We have no greater joy than to hear that our children walk in the truth." (KJV) Riding from place to place in those (or any) days changed dramatically whenever the preacher saw one of his converts or students living, teaching, or preaching what the preacher had taught. Seeing new converts grow to become preachers themselves warmed their hearts with a justifiable pride; a sense that their ministries had been worthwhile. Seeing a woman class member become class leader, perhaps to the point of being termed "a mother in Israel," had a similar effect. —Daniel P. Kidder, *The Christian Pastorate: Its Character, Responsibilities, and Duties.* Cincinnati: Hitchcock & Walden; New York: Carlton & Lanahan, 1871, 558&559.

The very best encouragement and reward, one which came in many forms and settings, was the boundless hope God provided. Hope for these preachers and for Methodists generally was never limited to a trite "I hope it's a nice day," or "I hope my business will succeed." Christian hope is larger than that, foundational and comprehensive. Hope is the basic orientation to life and eternity that is built upon the One we trust to lead us reliably along the road to glory. Hope is indispensable for getting through rough patches and celebrating milestones. Hope survives discouragement and outlasts pathetically empty distractions. Hope stands even at the grave, as it did with a friend of the dead Bishop Joseph Long, who said, "At the grave ... I felt as if I stood on holy ground, and the longing for my heavenly home was intensely quickened." —R. Yeakel, *Bishop Joseph Long.* Cleveland: Thomas & Matill, 1897, 123.

Thomas Morris beautifully described the length and depth Christian hope in one of his sermons:

> Well may the Christian's hope be called a glorious hope; for it is like "an anchor of the soul, both sure and steadfast, and which entereth into that within the vail," not the vail of the tabernacle, but of heaven, "where the forerunner is for us entered, even Jesus," our all in all. Let others seek their glory in the mansions of fame, or the fields of carnage; but, as one has said, "Our hope is not reared in earthly palaces; it dwells in the sanctuary of God; does not harness the chariot of conquest, nor spread the canopy of empire; but lives at the sick man's bed, and kneels down at the side of the tomb." "The righteous had hope in his death." And the hope we have in Jesus, cheers our lonesome hours, strengthens the weary and heavy laden, dries up the flowing tears of the lonely widow and her disconsolate orphans, brings the bread of life to the hungry poor, and enriches them with "gold tried in the fire;" softens the blows of affliction, hushes the storms of tribulation, pours the balm of love into the wounded spirit, lights the weary pilgrim to his grave, stands as his faithful sentinel till the morning of the resurrection, clothes him with the habiliments of immortality, and introduces him to the marriage supper of the Lamb, to regale himself with fruits which grow on the tree of life, where he may eat and live for ever. Lord, evermore give us this hope, through Jesus Christ our Lord. Amen.
> —T.A. Morris, "Hope," *Sermons on Various Subjects.* Cincinnati: Hitchcock & Walden; New York: Carlton & Lanahan, 1841, 102.

The ministry of old time circuit riders, their local counterparts, and the lay men and women who provided leadership, encouragement, discipline, and hospitality, could only have happened with resources like these: the inspiring presence of God; actual experiences of heaven, especially in worship, shaping and fortifying Christian hope; the wisdom and power of Scripture; peace, joy, and the other fruit of the Spirit; Christian literature, especially coming from authors and publishers in our tradition, including sermons and manuals; Christian friends and co-workers and their counsel; spouses and families, whose undying support came at great sacrifice; worship in such settings as camp meetings, class meetings, quarterly meetings, and other times of revival and renewal.

Greatest of all is the fountain, source, and guarantee of all hope; the "pioneer and perfecter of faith," the Lord of heaven and earth, the author of salvation, and our guide and goal on the road to glory. (Hebrews 12:2, NIV) Our Lord Jesus Christ lives within, inspires, and delivers all the other resources so necessary to ministry then and now.

CHAPTER 10

Transformation

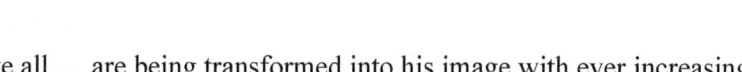

"And we all ... are being transformed into his image with ever increasing glory, which comes from the Lord, who is the Spirit." *II Corinthians 3:18, NIV*

"Changed from glory into glory, Till in heaven we take our place, Till we cast our crowns before they, Lost in wonder, love, and praise." Charles Wesley, "Love Divine, All Loves Excelling," *The African Methodist Episcopal Zion Hymnal.* Charlotte: A.M.E. Zion Publishing House, 1957, #408, v.4.

For those in the Methodist tradition, conversion was never a "once and done" experience, a transaction resulting in legal acquittal and a ticket to heaven. Instead, it was a complete reorientation, a radical new start, but not an immediate finish. Conversion began the long process of transformation leading to Christian perfection and a place in God's new creation. That transformation had to be deep and thorough, producing a new person, whose life was joined forever with Christ, empowered by the Holy Spirit, and actively engaged in a trajectory leading toward an eternal destiny. It was and is participation in the very nature of God, as Peter put it in his second letter. (II Peter 1:4, NIV) At the same time, it is becoming who we really are, fulfilling our purpose and destiny, restoring God's image within our souls, without taking away our distinct and meaningful identity as his creatures. Without in any way devaluing our participation in this life we've been given, sanctification is headed somewhere else, somewhere that will bring this life to its never-ending perfection.

Twentieth-century evangelist E. Stanley Jones pointed to the secret of this kind of radical transformation, which plumbed the depths and reached into the core of people's lives. This was no superficial improvement, but a change of heart that produced a changed life and destiny: "If you open your life to the depths, then He will make you over at the depth. He will do as thorough a work as you will allow him to do." —E. Stanley Jones, *Growing Spiritually.* New York, NY & Nashville, TN: Abingdon, 1953, 25.

Phillip William Otterbein spoke of the victory of the cross being more than external; more than a superficial transaction. Instead, that victory must, by grace and with our cooperation, work its way thoroughly into the depths of our lives in a complete process of sanctification, finally defeating the remnants of Satan's power and our cooperation with that power.

> He who relies upon grace stays with Jesus ... proceeds onward. Growth is a sign of a person's standing in grace, and strengthens the heart. Indeed, the higher the degree of godly life that a person reaches in this time, the firmer is the hope that he also has for that future openness and joy in God. —Phillip William Otterbein, "The Salvation-Bringing Incarnation and the Glorious Victory of Jesus Christ over the Devil and Death Delivered" (Sermon, published in 1763), in J. Steven O'Malley, *Early German-American Evangelicalism.* Lanham, MD & London, UK: Scarecrow, 1995, 33.

Raymond Albright recognized the limits of ordinary church life and worship to reach masses of German people, even with the far-flung network of circuits and their preachers. Their efforts were greatly enlarged and deepened by the instrumentality of camp meetings, by which Evangelicals and United Brethren, as well as "English" Methodists, gathered people from considerable distances. "These camp meetings came to be considered sacred, for many were converted there." John Dreisbach said of one meeting, held in 1818, "Never did I hear the brethren deliver better, more instructive and energetic sermons than at this camp meeting. Sinners were awakened and converted, and the children of God greatly edified and advanced in the work of grace." —Raymond W. Albright, *A History of the Evangelical Church.* Harrisburg: Evangelical Press, 1942, 156-158.

The point of all this preaching, whatever shape it took, was to advance the entire panorama of grace in people's lives, from initial conviction and justification through the process of sanctification and readiness for eternity. Class and band meetings, outdoor camp meetings and indoor revivals, spiritual reading and conversation, and worship in local congregations were all meant to make and grow disciples by accessing grace for eager, receptive people. No obstacle, from physical confrontations to intellectual resistance; from geographic separation to cultural barriers, could stop these efforts, or at least their honest attempts, to open a way for grace to fill and transform.

Erwin House describes transformation as "soul growth," which is "the growth of a soul in virtues, in usefulness, in assimilation to God...." Soul growth is endless, for it is always approaching the unapproachable, which is likeness to God, the image of God. This is the growth that begins in this life as we enter the kingdom through faith, and then continues into the endless expanses of eternity. Thus, death "is not the extinction of your being, it is not the suspension of your powers, it is not even the interruption of your progress; the soul is renewed day by day." All of this is why transformation produces endless hope. —Erwin House, *The Homilist*. New York: Carlton & Lanahan; San Francisco: E. Thomas; Cincinnati: Hitchcock & Walden, 1860, 224-226.

For those who opposed Christianity and/or its Methodist expressions, it would take a great jolt to change their hearts and minds. Such a jolt came for a lawyer who had made a reputation as a contentious unbeliever. It came in the form of two terrible deaths of local men who had rejected the Christian message, and then died horrible deaths, believing their cases were hopeless. The second "lamentable death," like the first, "produced a powerful sensation in the community. Among the fruits thereof was the conversion of an infidel lawyer of the town." This man was committed enough to his position that "he had held public debates in the town with an Episcopal clergyman, against the Bible." For whatever reason, the lawyer attended a protracted meeting at which William Reeves, a Methodist preacher, "had aimed many a blow at his infidel system.... Yet this man appeared to be armed with a coat of mail, and seemed to be able to resist all the arguments that came from the pulpit."

But news of the latest death "roused up all his powers of reflection," and got hold of his heart, breaking through his "coat of mail." He went to the preacher with his lack of faith badly shaken, ready "to see Christianity in altogether a new light." At the Reeves' invitation, he sat with those who were "seekers of religion."

> Several evenings after this, ...this gentleman asked permission of Mr. Reeves to speak. Of course it was readily granted. He then arose and addressed the audience, renounced his infidelity, and openly declared his conversion to Christianity in thrilling utterances, never to be forgotten. He then appealed to the church members for an interest in their prayers, that he might be able, by the grace of God, to convince the community, not by his statements and professions alone, but his reformed and exemplary life, that there is a divine reality in experimental ["Known by experience; having personal experience."] religion.

His arguments melted before the horror of, even at second hand, seeing people die without faith, without hope, and knowing how different it was for Christians. George Brown, retelling this story, wrote, "All must see the utter futility of infidelity in the dying hour, and that it takes Christianity to make life happy, death triumphant, and eternity glorious." —George Brown, *The Lady Preacher.* Philadelphia: Daughaday & Becker; Springfield, OH: Methodist Publishing House, 1870, 242-245; Noah Webster, *An American Dictionary of the English Language.* Springfield, MA: George & Charles Merriam, 1848, 424.

The allure of skepticism is real, and some can live in the world of clashing ideas for many years without reality breaking in and their house of cards collapsing. Faced constantly by the reality of death in those early days, some would see the impossibility of making sense out of life "without hope and without God in the world." (Ephesians 2:12, NIV) What is really encouraging about this story is the man's willingness – eagerness, really – to prove, by grace, the reality of his transformation.

Transformation in this life prefigures and leads to further transformation in the life to come – a transformation of spirit, but also of body. Paul wrote in Philippians that "the Lord Jesus Christ, who by the power that enables him to bring everything under his control, will transform our lowly bodies so that they will be like his glorious body." (Philippians 3:20&21, NIV) James Finley spoke of this in connection with the death of a colleague, I.C. Hunter.

> Trusting alone in the merits of Jesus, he entered the valley and was lost to earth, but was found in heaven. His body lies in a quiet, peaceful rural cemetery, near the town of Burlington, on the Ohio river. There, undisturbed, may his ashes rest till the archangel shall wake them into that new and beautiful form which the saints shall have at the resurrection! —W.P. Strickland, ed., *Autobiography of Rev. James B. Finley.* Cincinnati: Methodist Book Concern, 1855, 272&273.

Transformation gives practical significance for this life to our Christian beliefs about the next. Resurrection power is seen in Jesus, and also in his people, who have trusted his promise that "Because I live, you also will live." (John 14:19, NIV) In our individual lives, transformation does not wait for death to remove us from this world, but works in us by the power of the Spirit to prepare us for our transition to the new world.

The living, daily reality of sanctifying grace in our lives deepens our appreciation for key realities included in the historic creeds. The experience of transformation and the presence of heaven in worship take us well beyond merely believing as a matter of affirmation. The Nicene Creed says it well: "We *look for* the resurrection of the dead, and the life of the world to come." Looking for resurrection is an active, eager pursuit of an actual occurrence, not merely a belief that it will happen. When the

Apostles' Creed says "I believe in ... the resurrection of the body and the life everlasting," it is affirming what we already experience, though only in part, on the road to glory. Resurrection and everlasting life will not only happen *to* us, but are already happening *in* us. —*The United Methodist Hymnal.* Nashville: The United Methodist Publishing House, 1989, #s 880 & 881, with my italics.

The process of transformation flowed from the various means of grace available to our early movement. All the forms of revival, from regional camp and quarterly meetings, to class and protracted meetings in local settings, to Sunday school and daily personal prayer, were designed to initiate and nurture every stage in a grace-filled life. At quarterly meetings, for example, while experienced Christians "renewed our covenants with God and his people, obtained encouragement and strength in our souls, and rejoiced together in the salvation of God," those beginning to sense a need for God "found hope by seeing peers who, in all respects, were like themselves yet could testify to the transformation power of God's grace in their lives." —David Lewis in Lester Ruth, *A Little Heaven Below: Worship at Early Methodist Quarterly Meetings.* Nashville: Kingswood (Abingdon), 2000, 183; 173.

The New Testament is very specific on the marks of a transformed life. II Peter lists several, which, while connected to each other, may or may not be given in sequence: "For this very reason, make every effort to add to your faith goodness; and to goodness, knowledge; and to knowledge, self-control; and to self-control, perseverance; and to perseverance, godliness; and to godliness, mutual affection; and to mutual affection, love." These characteristics should appear "in increasing measure," for if someone's life proves "ineffective and unproductive," that person has lost sight of the road that should lead from initial forgiveness to participation "in the divine nature." (II Peter 1:4-9, NIV)

The Letters of John speak of walking in love, which "comes from God," and should show itself in our relationships with others. II and III John stress "walking in the truth," which means not only obeying Jesus' command to love, but reflecting the One who is love in our own character and behavior. (I John 4:7; II John vs. 4&6; III John v. 4; John 13:34; 14:6, NIV)

Philippians speaks of humility that imitates Jesus, and Paul tells the Colossians to "clothe yourselves with compassion, kindness, humility, gentleness, and patience. Bear with each other and forgive whatever grievances you may have against one another. Forgive as the Lord forgave you. And over all these virtues put on love, which binds them all together in perfect unity." (Philippians 2:3-8; Colossians 3: NIV)

Galatians lists "the fruit of the Spirit" and tells us to "keep in step with the Spirit;" to "serve one another in love" because "The entire law is summed up in a single command: 'Love your neighbor as yourself.'" (Galatians 5:22; 25; 13&14, NIV).

All these attitudes and behaviors build toward perfect love, which is made possible only by grace and which aligns our souls and character with the Spirit and character of God. They follow and accompany a progressive abandonment of sin and selfishness, from the first conviction that something is seriously wrong in one's life, through forgiveness, conversion, and new life, and on to every step of sanctification. Movement from one to another of these stages must be continual. George Peck wrote, "Any foundation, be it ever so firmly laid, if left unoccupied, will very soon go to decay, and finally become a mass of ruins. So the mere elements of Christian character will soon be lost, unless we proceed to advanced ground." —George Peck, *The Scripture Doctrine of Christian Perfection.* New-York: Carlton & Phillips, 1854, 15.

This is why both James and Paul wrote of endurance over time and victory over adversity, a theme in Jesus' own teaching. In James, we see progress from faith, through testing, to perseverance, to completion and "the crown of life." The opposite pattern is desire, leading to sin, leading on to death. (James 1:3&4; 12, NIV) Paul urged the putting on of various kinds of spiritual armor, so that "you may be able to stand your ground, and after you have done everything, to stand." In Romans we are called to "rejoice in the hope of the glory of God," even in times of suffering, because those experiences are only the beginning of our progress toward that glory, for "suffering produces perseverance; perseverance, character; and character, hope." Once our grace-empowered efforts toward perseverance have proven and strengthened themselves, they are transformed into our character or identity. They become who we are in Christ. (Ephesians 6:13, NIV; Romans 5:2-4, NIV) Final salvation comes not with conversion, but with grace building our character, and finally "the one who stands firm to the end will be saved." (Mark 13:13, NIV) This is the vision expressed in Jesus' words from the Sermon on the Mount: "Be perfect, therefore, as your heavenly Father is perfect." (Matthew 5:48, NIV) These more than challenging words resemble those in in I Peter: "Be holy, because I am holy." (I Peter 1:16, NIV; Cf. Leviticus 11:44&45; 19:2)

Although our willing cooperation is required for all of this, it is always at God's initiative and by his power. We are not just becoming somewhat better people, or making gradual improvements to our personalities, at God's command. Instead, Paul says "we ... are being transformed into his [Christ's] likeness with ever-increasing glory, which comes from the Lord, who is the Spirit." (II Corinthians 3:18, NIV) God intends for each of us to be "a new creation," living for him and not for ourselves, prepared for "an eternal house in heaven," which we will receive from God. (II Corinthians 5:17; 15; 1, NIV) The implications for the way we look at life as we move through the years are staggering. Such a radical change means:

> Though outwardly we are wasting away, yet inwardly we are being renewed day by day. For our light and momentary troubles are achieving for us an eternal glory that far outweighs them all. So we fix our eyes not on what is seen, but on what is unseen, since what is seen is temporary, but what is unseen is eternal. (II Corinthians 4:16-18, NIV)

No wonder these verses were used so often by our preacher ancestors! The transformation of our selves, our characters, to be conformed to the image of God in Christ, so that the very life of God lives within us, is an astonishing opportunity, and it was this opportunity that preachers in our tradition accepted and sought to communicate. —To explore this area further, see S.T. Kimbrough, Jr., *Partakers of the Divine Nature.* Eugene, OR: Cascade, 2016; Henry H. Knight III, *Anticipating Heaven Below.* Eugene, OR: Cascade, 2014; Thomas C. Oden, *The Transforming Power of Grace.* Nashville: Abingdon, 1993; Mildred Bangs Wynkoop, *A Theology of Love (etc.).* Kansas City, MO: Beason Hill, 1972.

First steps in this journey were often taken at camp meetings, when people were presented with the dangers and promises of eternity. Peter Cartwright was set free from overwhelming guilt and distress and soundly converted at one of the earliest camp meetings in America, a "sacramental meeting" connected with Cane Ridge.

> To this meeting I repaired, a guilty, wretched sinner. On the Saturday evening of said meeting I went, with weeping multitudes, and bowed before the stand, and earnestly prayed for mercy. In the midst of a solemn struggle of soul, an impression was made on my mind, as though a voice said to me, "Thy sins are all forgiven thee." Divine light flashed all round me, unspeakable joy sprung up in my soul. I rose to my feet, opened my eyes, and it really seemed as if I was in heaven; the trees, the leaves on them, and every thing seemed, and I really thought were, praising God. —W.P. Strickland, ed., *Autobiography of Peter Cartwright.* New York: Phillips & Hunt; Cincinnati: Walden & Stowe, 1856, 37.

Here was the beginning of a lifetime of growth in grace and ministry. The depth to which the Spirit reached in the souls of converts shows both the depth of sin that had to be addressed and overcome, and the power of God to accomplish change at that level, from the inside out. Often when people prayed through, they experienced a peace as powerful as the turmoil they had known.

Cartwright wrote of the drastic changes that sometimes followed a transforming encounter with God. At one camp meeting, "hundreds fell to the ground, and scores of souls were happily born into the kingdom of God that afternoon and during the night." As a result, one family "set their slaves free, and the end of that family was peace."

John Seybert wrote about a Pennsylvania camp meeting held by the Evangelical Association, where Henry Fisher was the preacher. When the invitation came for people to pray at the altar,

> The people cried out in loud lamentations, fairly staggering toward the altar, pleading for mercy in their helpless distress. Even in the outskirts of the audience, the spiritually wounded began to tremble and quake, and cry out. They wrung their hands in agony, or smote upon their breast, wailing, "God, be merciful to me a sinner". In the multitude sat a woman with a child in her arm, who trembled and wept so sorely in her appalling spiritual grief, that by-standers relieved her of the child while she tottered to the altar.
>
> The sisters encouraged her all they could, until she found peace in the Redeemer. She was wondrously changed. The very fashion of her countenance was altered. —John Seybert, in S.P. Spreng, *The Life and Labors of John Seybert.* Cleveland: Lauer & Matill, 1888, 147&148.

We may find stories like these strange. The level of emotion may appear extreme, and the exercise of God's power in people's lives may come across as exaggerated or difficult to believe. However, stories like these are extremely common in circuit rider literature, and the lives of countless transformed people witness to their reality and durability. As we look at the role of worship on the road to glory, we will see that the source of the transformation that happened in revival settings was not the emotion or the eloquence of preachers, though these were certainly present. But deeper and stronger than any human agency was the outpouring of the Holy Spirit, often coming in a collapse of any barrier separating earth from heaven.

CHAPTER 11

Worship

"On the Lord's Day I was in the Spirit...." —*Revelation 1:10, NIV*

"Anticipate your heaven below...." —Charles Wesley, "O For a Thousand Tongues to Sing," *The United Methodist Hymnal.* Nashville: The United Methodist Publishing House, 1989, #57, v. 7.

Worship was the life blood of Wesleyan Christians in their early years in North America. Whether in church buildings or remote cabins; in congregations, camp meetings, or conferences, Methodists experienced God's power, forgiveness, and wisdom amid the fellowship of his people. In worship they found renewing, empowering grace for their journey of faith. Worship brought together most of the resources that fed into people's understanding and experience of heaven – Scripture, prayer, fellowship, Eucharist, testimony, and most of all, the undeniable, transforming, and often surprising presence and power of God. At outdoor gatherings these things happened away from the distraction of ordinary routines and in the midst of God's creation.

James K. A. Smith says, "The church's worship is a uniquely intense site of the Spirit's transformative presence (James K. A. Smith, *You Are What You Love.* Grand Rapids, MI: Brazos, 2016, 70)." God's "transformative presence" is exactly what early Methodists were seeking, and seeking to share with others. They found in worship that which they searched for, which gave them life and equipped them for their mission. Theirs was the longing expressed in Psalm 63: "You, God, are my God, earnestly I seek you; I thirst for you, my whole being longs for you, in a dry and weary land where there is no water. I have seen you in the sanctuary and beheld your power and your glory." (Psalm 63:1&2, NIV)

Often, though not automatically, and never to be taken for granted, worship brought heaven to earth. Hannah Reeves showed the connection between heaven and earth in worship as she gave a funeral sermon. "She appeared to be raised far above herself that day. God certainly spoke through her to the people, so that the expansion of thought, and the power and beauty of language, all seemed to be right from Heaven." —George Brown, *The Lady Preacher.* Philadelphia: Daughaday & Becher; Springfield, OH: Methodist Publishing House, 1870, 69.

Charles Giles helps us understand how pioneers discovered the full reality and depth of worship, apart from the presence of purpose-built churches. It is a discovery that many have come to share when we have needed to worship in times that swept away what we had relied upon as normal. As he does this, Giles takes us to the highest point of worship, the experience of glory, as heaven itself descends to earth and God is in the midst of his people, even while they are making their way to eternity:

> At that time there were no churches erected within the bounds of our extensive circuit. Indeed, there was only one Methodist church in all this western country, except for a few temporary log buildings. Hence we were under the necessity of preaching in school-houses, private rooms, barns, or in the wilderness. These humble places being the best accommodations the condition of the country could then afford, all appeared to be contented and even thankful for the privileges they enjoyed. Pure spiritual worship which emanates from the pious heart, can be offered acceptably in any place; and wherever Christ meets his worshipping saints, there is peace, paradise, and heaven. What is earthly splendour? – nothing! But to seek for and obtain heavenly glory, honour, immortality, eternal life, is everything – the essence and sublimity of all perfection. —Charles Giles, *Pioneer.* New-York: G. Lane & P.P. Sandford, 1844, 138.

Canadian Methodist Joseph Hilts, who attended many camp meetings, including the one at which he was converted, wrote about what these events meant to him, and the way people were lifted up toward heaven:

> If there is any place on this earth that is more like heaven than a good live camp-meeting, I should like to hear from it. I would be pleased to know where it is, and on what grounds the claim is made. To commune with nature is, to a devout mind, a precious privilege. To commune with good people is a blessed means of grace. And to commune with God is a greater blessing than either of these. To hold converse with nature, tends to expand the intellect and quicken the sensibilities. To hold friendly intercourse with the good elevates, refines, and stimulates the social and moral elements of our being. And to commune with God purifies and exalts our whole nature, and inspires us to a holier life and loftier aims and a fuller consecration to the service of God.

... I know of no place where the ethical, esthetical, social and spiritual wants of humanity are more fully provided for than at the camp-meeting. There some of the most soul-inspiring scenes that earth can furnish may be witnessed. When a strong religious influence is felt by the assembled worshippers as, with cheerful voices they ring out the melody of their gladdened hearts, where is the soul so dead as not to feel an impulse drawing heavenward? The trees that surround this leafy temple seem to catch the spirit of song, and send back to the ears of the happy worshippers in pleasing echoes the very words they are giving utterance to. ... Even the shadows cast by the trees and limbs that intercept the lights of the camp-fires seem to enter into the spirit of the occasion, and point upward to a realm where darkness is unheard of and shadows are unknown. —Joseph H. Hilts, *Experiences of a Backwoods Preacher.* Wiarton, ON: Bruce County Historical Society, 1984, 95&96.

AME preacher Thomas W. Henry wrote about meetings he held on a farm in Maryland. These gathering took place on land owned by Casper Weaver, an architect and executive for the Baltimore and Ohio Railroad. Weaver ran interference for Henry, promising that no one would disturb these meetings, an important consideration given that some whites were trying to shut down services held by African Americans. Brother Henry described his experience at these meetings, which brought participants together from great distances as they brought heaven to earth:

The Lord blessed me on this occasion, and it seems that He blessed nearly everybody that came there. The people met together from every direction. They came from the lower part of the Maryland tract and up the Potomac on the Maryland side, from Harper's Ferry, and a great many from a considerable distance in Virginia, to our Christmas and Easter meetings, which were more like camp-meetings. I often thought to myself, and it looked just that way to me, that a heaven on earth had begun. We went on there with these meetings for about five years, with these good blessings attending us during that time; and I am thankful to say, God was with us. —Jean Libby, ed., *From Slavery to Salvation: The Autobiography of Rev. Thomas W. Henry, of the A.M.E. Church.* Jackson, MS: University Press of Mississippi, 1994, 31&32.

Andrew Carroll explained the nature of a camp meeting to his friends in Ireland, where he originated. After describing the arrangement of the camp ground, he explained: "These camp meetings are the paradise of believers, yea, the borderland of heaven. To repenting sinners they become the means of introducing them to the Fountain that cleanses from unrighteousness, and prepares them for the society of the blessed." —Andrew Carroll, *Moral and Religious Sketches and Collections.* Cincinnati: Methodist Book Concern, 1857, 38.

Hard as it may be for us to imagine, Conferences held much the same spiritual power and fellowship as camp meetings. Quarterly Meetings, Annual and General Conferences drew impressive crowds not so much to argue and transact, but to celebrate and renew. When Methodists gathered for Conference, along with necessary business, "they devoted themselves to the apostles' teaching and to fellowship, to the breaking of bread and to prayer (Acts 2:42, NIV)."

John H. Day's presiding elder, A.N. Fillmore, arrived, after much difficulty, to lead a fall quarterly meeting on a mountainous Pennsylvania circuit: "Its scenery was wild and majestic, with deep, rich, arable valleys set in the framework of high mountains. ... They received me as kindly as though I had been an angel from heaven." Fillmore reached the remote site of the meeting,

> amid the storms and almost impassible roads. ... He had forded the streams and breasted the tempests. In looking out upon the boiling waters of the Big Sock and up to the mountains piled toward the clouds, he said, 'It was the wildest and most sublime scene I had ever witnessed.' 'Who can get here?' was the question. But at the hour, by the use of boats, they came, representative men from nearly every appointment. A fair congregation assembled, and the Lord crowned the meeting with his presence and blessing. —F.G. Hibbard, *History of the Late East Genesee Conference of the Methodist Episcopal Church.* New York: Phillips & Hunt, 1887, 95-97.

Why would a presiding elder brave that kind of travel just to convene a quarterly meeting? Why would brother Day navigate such a demanding circuit in order to reach one remote settlement after another? Why would representatives from those settlements sail on "the boiling waters of the Big Sock" to attend such a meeting? It was because quarterly meeting was, most of all, a meeting between God and his people, a foretaste of the perfect worship they longed for in heaven.

Charles Giles said of one quarterly meeting: "Indeed, the place seemed like the gate of heaven; though the building in which we worshipped was only a rough barn, it was honoured with the presence of God." —Charles Giles, *Pioneer.* New-York: G. Lane & P.P. Sandford, 1844, 86.

F.G. Hibbard wrote, "The Annual Conference is the great central home-gathering of the social life to its members." These were times of renewal of spirit and friendship among the traveling preachers. Conferences in that day were times of revival, as well as decision making. Here pastors who had been scattered across the face of the earth were reunited and reinvigorated for their work. Here they shared their stories of trials and victories, or new lives and new congregations. From here they would return to their circuits or begin new assignments. For many preachers, conference was a rare constant in the midst of constant change. Here preachers could open their hearts to each other in full confidence that their conversation partners knew what it was like. —F.G. Hibbard, *History of the East Genesee Conference.* New York: Phillips & Hunt, 1887, 165.

Henry Smith remembered going to the Methodist Episcopal General Conference in 1804, and, specifically, what it was like to meet "William Burke, James Quinn, and others from the West.... Our meeting was unexpected but joyful; for who can describe the satisfaction of meeting old soldiers of the cross who have labored and suffered together for years! —Henry Smith, *Recollections and Reflections of an Old Itinerant.* New-York: Carlton & Phillips, 1854, 126.

Quarterly Meetings brought preachers and people together from smaller regions in an experience that bears little resemblance to the Charge Conferences or congregational meetings of today. George Peck wrote of sermons, baptisms, and Eucharistic celebration as part of that experience. There was the sharing of testimonies and mutual encouragement. Quarterly meetings attracted Methodists and guests from a given region and extended across several days, usually led by the Presiding Elder for that district.

On the frontier,

> Barns, for many years after this, were common places for the holding of quarterly meetings. Many a barn ... has been sanctified by the presence and power of God, and been the spiritual birthplace of precious souls. ... The people came from afar to attend them, and returned home full of the Holy Ghost and of faith. —George Peck, *Early Methodism within the Bounds of the Old Genesee Conference.* New York: Carlton & Porter, 1860, 205; 64.

It became common for those swept up in the fire of revival to undergo radical changes in attitude and behavior. The power of those meetings shook many to the foundation of their being and made them new people. One episode in John Seybert's ministry was typical, as "thousands who had come into the congregation simultaneously fell upon their knees, and devoutly joined in worshipping God. It was an impressive and overpowering scene. ... The outcries and groans of poor sinners, mingled with the shouts of God's people over their deliverance rose to an extraordinary height, and continue until the dawn of the next morning." —S.P. Spreng, *The Life and Labors of John Seybert.* Cleveland, OH: Lauer & Matill, 1888, 165. Peter Cartwright wrote of two jealous suitors, determined to kill each other over the woman they loved, who were actually reconciled at the altar as "many fell under the preaching of the word." One of those men later became a preacher.

> There was a remarkable instance of the power of religion manifested in the change of these two young men. A few hours before they were sworn enemies, thirsting for each other's blood, but now all those murderous feelings were removed from them, and, behold! their hearts were filled with love. "Old things were done away, and all things became new." —W.P. Strickland, ed. *Autobiography of Peter Cartwright, The Backwoods Preacher.* New York: Philllips & Hunt; Cincinnati: Walden & Stowe, 1856, 239.

Reflecting on the fluid, white hot situation of earliest Methodism, David Smith, one of the first AME circuit riders, recalled preaching to black and also to mixed congregations, with excellent results. On one occasion, he led a Methodist Episcopal gathering that included "slaves and their owners singing, shouting, and praising God together" in a fragile foretaste of worship in heaven. He said, amazingly,

> All seemed to be one in Christ Jesus; there was no distinction as to the rich or poor, bond or free, but all were melted into sweet communion with the spirit (sic) and united in Christian fellowship; and to my mind they could have befittingly sang the blessed hymn:
>
> "Blessed by the dear uniting love
> That will not let us part;
> Our bodies may far off remove,
> We still are one in heart." —David Smith, *Biography of Rev. David Smith.* n.c.: n.p., 1881, -10; See Charles Wesley, "Blest Be the Dear Uniting Love," *African Methodist Episcopal Church Hymnal.* Nashville: The African Methodist Episcopal Church, 1984, #527, v.1.

How could such unlikely experiences occur at that early time? They happened when people of various ethnic and economic backgrounds were so thoroughly and powerfully swept up in the spirit of revival that in that moment, nothing else, not even the most grievous injustices, mattered enough to get in the way. These were times when women and African Americans could speak – even preach, pray, offer testimony, and respond to invitations without creating the kind of reactions that would too soon become normal. They happened when people were drawn so deeply into the heart of God that such distinctions could be temporarily put aside. We could wish that they had been removed and put aside permanently, but even these brief encounters at the throne of grace are remarkable in themselves, and serve as pioneering models for our own ongoing struggles with multicultural worship. The reason revivals, especially camp meetings, which were held away from anyone's church building, could have this ability, is the presence and power of God that in certain moments overcame every other consideration.

Benjamin Titus Roberts described a meeting in western New York where "there were five slain under the power of God," a new experience for some in that place, but common, especially in camp meetings, across the country. To Roberts this was a sign of God's power in the midst of worship. Lamenting the demise of high intensity worship once part of the older quarterly meetings, Henry Boehm said in 1875, "There was power among the fathers, both in the ministry and laity, that we do not possess. The ministers moved the masses as the wind does a field of wheat, and they mowed them down as the scythe does the grass. —Benson Howard Roberts, *Benjamin Titus Roberts*. North Chili, NY: Earnest Christian, 1900, 85; Henry Boehm, in Lester Ruth, *A Little Heaven Below: Worship at Early Methodist Quarterly Meetings*. Nashville: Kingswood (Abingdon), 2005, 184.

Billy Hibbard wrote about this phenomenon at early camp meetings:

> Many are so wrought upon, that they are deprived of their strength and fall to the ground. Various opinions were formed respecting this work; some said "they were weak minds only who were wrought upon in this manner."
> ...
> But it was generally known that the change wrought in those weak men and women, so called, made them very religious. And as they were known to lead pious lives afterwards, it was then thought to be a good means to reform weak minds. Such was the opinion of those who felt themselves above being religious in a humble manner. —Billy Hibbard, *Memoirs of the Life and Travels of B. Hibbard.* n.c.: B. Hibbard, 1825, 294&295.

There will be more about such phenomena in a later chapter. For now, these typical stories reveal the capacity of worship to move people deeply enough to shake them to their shoes, reorient their lives, and start or restart them on the road to glory.

Similar to camp and the earliest quarterly meetings, Primitive Methodists attended field meetings, where "realizing sense of the presence of God" would come in the midst of prayers, preaching, singing, and fellowship. These field meetings gathered people in an outdoor venue that brought them together, apart from their normal surroundings and schedules, into the transforming presence of God. In their distance from the ordinary, they prepared for a life beyond this one, which they could glimpse even in a present moment. —Mrs. R.P Hopper, *Old-time Primitive Methodism in Canada (1829-1884)*. Toronto: William Briggs, 1904, 119.

Charles Giles describes a Communion service where the power of God was very much in evidence. His description shows that power descending upon an outdoor celebration of the Lord's Supper, which followed an already powerful time of preaching and response:

> At the same time the divine Spirit was operating on all around, which was evidently seen in the devout appearance of the congregation. But when the solemn sacramental scene was opened, it seemed that heaven was opened at the same time, and filled the wilderness where we were assembled with unearthly glory. Joyful exclamations, tears, and dread, all conspired to tell, emphatically, that the God of salvation was there. Among these happy worshippers there was a Presbyterian deacon, who said to me afterward, that it seemed to him he could almost hear the angels sing and rejoice with us while we were celebrating the Saviour's love at the communion table.
> —Charles Giles, *Pioneer.* New-York: G. Lane & P.P. Sandford, 1844, 178.

The Methodist class meeting, which John Carroll called "this social means of grace," provided the oversight – today we would say accountability - and encouragement people needed to continue, in good times and bad, along the road of transformation and glory. While class meetings declined in some churches later in the nineteenth century, their revival in the twenty-first is testimony to their enduring value. Class meetings provided small group worship and fellowship leading to their longed for destiny. Like worship generally, class meetings were "our heaven below." —John Carroll, *The Stripling Preacher or a Sketch of the Life and Character ... of the Rev. Alexander S. Byrne.* Toronto: Anson Green, 1852, 13; Ebenezer Hills, *hymn quoted in Lester Ruth, Early Methodist Life and Spirituality.* Nashville: Kingswood (Abingdon), 2005, 144.

James P. Horton wrote of a class meeting at which "Floods of glory, and light, from heaven came pouring in upon us from the upper world."— James P. Horton, *A Narrative of the Early Life, Remarkable Conversion, and Spiritual Labors of James P. Horton.* n.c: Printed for the Author, 1839, 203.

Whether in camp, quarterly, or class meetings; in local churches or regional gatherings, worship brought heaven and the power of God to earth, in the midst of his people. Worship gave believers a foretaste of heaven, and heaven fulfilled that foretaste. Thus John Lewis Dyer could describe heaven as "that better country, where congregations are large, and never break-up." Reflecting his own experience, he could imagine the worship of those "with whom I shared privations, dangers, and religious joys in the Rocky Mountains." —John Lewis Dyer, *The Snow-Shoe Itinerant.* Cincinnati: Cranston & Stowe, 1890, 209.

John Newton's hymn, "As When the Weary Traveler Gains," gives us the image of the Christian on a journey, one which affords from time to time a vantage point from which travelers can see their destination, and in that seeing, find hope and strength.

> As when the weary traveler gains
> The height of some commanding hill
> His heart revives, if 'cross the plains,
> He sees his home, though distant still. —John Newton, *"As When the Weary Traveler Gains,"* in *Hymns for the Sanctuary.* Dayton: United Brethren Publishing House, 1879, #1133, v. 1.

That vantage point, which "His heart revives," was often "gain[ed]" in times of worship.

"Ezekiel Cooper once described a 1790 Baltimore worship service as the 'suburbs of heaven.'" Similarly, William Watters said after another service, 'I was as in a little Heaven below, and believe Heaven above will differ more in quantity that in quality.'" As with Eastern Orthodox sanctuaries in a different worship culture, when they entered a camp ground, they were entering the kingdom, even if only for a day or a week. Whether bringing heaven to earth or lifting people up to heaven, worship in such settings broke through the barrier between two kingdoms. Early Methodists saw heaven as an extension of what they were experiencing in worship here, so that worship was a taste of eternal life. —Russell E. Richey, *Methodism in the American Forest.* Oxford & New York, et al., Oxford University Press, 2015, 131; Lester Ruth, *Early Methodist Life and Spirituality.* Nashville: Kingswood (Abingdon), 2005, 136.

Those who try to analyze such gatherings by looking only at the arrangements of the camp grounds, or the schedules that were followed, or the demographics of those who participated, or even the motivation of those who attended, will fail to understand what was happening. A list of hymns, Scripture texts, sermon outlines, or the personalities of the preachers, will fall hopelessly short of reality. Yet the recollections of participants can take us there. They can re-create in our imaginations something of what it *felt like* to be on the grounds. But more importantly, they invite us to see the kingdom, perhaps even for a moment to enter it, and to realize that what was happening there outshone any attempt to reduce it to words, procedures, or psychology.

In fact, Jonas Peck warned that "in too many revivals, it must be confessed, there is too much dependence on this human machinery, and too little reliance on the dynamics of our holy religion." On the basis of his own observation and study, Peck concluded,

> From the patient study of the subject of revival power in Christian history the conviction will strengthen that the Church is tending in the wrong

direction when it multiplies and depends so much upon machinery, and seems to realize so little its absolute helplessness without divine power. ... ...without this power from on high all machinery is useless. —Jonas Oramel Peck, *The Revival and the Pastor.* New York: Hunt & Eaton; Cincinnati: Cranston & Curts, 1894, 82-84; 93.

James P. Horton described vividly his own experience in worship at a love feast, in a way that demonstrates its depth and power.

> ... my soul was so filled with the love of God, that for some time I was lost to all that was passing around me. It appeared to me that I was taken up into heaven, and there I saw the Lord upon his great white throne, and he spoke to me in melting language, thus: 'Behold, dear child, none but the pure in heart can come here.' And there I saw the shining happy millions flaming around his throne in such immortal beauty that my tongue cannot describe it. If I had really been translated to glory, it appeared to me I could not have been happier. When I came to my recollection, I was standing upon my seat with my hands uplifted, and when I looked down upon the people around me, they looked like the shining ones in whose company I seemed to be the moment before in the heavenly world. —James P. Horton, in Lester Ruth, *Early Methodist Life and Spirituality.* Nashville: Kingswood (Abingdon), 2005, 145.

George White tried to relate what he experienced when, at a meeting in his home, "I fell prostrate upon the floor, like one dead." This experience became common in revivals, especially camp meetings, where an individual or even hundreds at once would be struck down in the midst of worship, often to rise to a new dimension of life. What is less common is a clear description of what it was like for someone going through that experience, especially with the clarity of White's statement:

> But while I lay in this condition, my mind was vigorous and active; and an increasing scene of glory, opened upon my ravished soul; with a spiritual view of the heavenly hosts surrounding the eternal throne, giving glory to God and the Lamb; with whom, all my ransomed powers seemed to unite, in symphonious strains of divine adoration; feeling nothing but perfect love[,] peace, joy, and goodwill to man, pervading all my soul, in a most happy union with God, my all in all – every doubt[,] fear and terror of mind were banished, and heaven opened in my bosom.

White's response to this strange, powerful encounter with the heavenly realm was not to revel in the warmth of positive emotion, nor to return to his usual self, unchanged. He described his vision in language far from individualistic escapism, but as a "divine manifestation of the power of sanctifying grace," empowering him for greater ministry:

> ...from this time, what had before appeared like insurmountable difficul-

ties, were now made easy, by casting my whole care upon the Lord; and the path of duty was only the path of pleasure. I could pray without ceasing, and rejoice evermore; and my stammering tongue was more than ever loosed, to declare the truth of God, with greater zeal, and affection. At the same time that I received this inestimable blessing, there were many others who were awakened, converted, and made happy in the pardoning love of Christ. The memory of that glorious day will never be erased from my mind. —Graham Russell Hodges, ed., *Black Itinerants of the Gospel: The Narratives of John Jea and George White,* New York: Palgrave, 2002, 58.

This was an experience so radical and compelling that it changed his life forever. When experiences like this were shared, they could break down barriers that would customarily have divided the participants. Was it a vision, or an actual experience of heaven? Given the transcendence of boundaries separating the kingdoms of earth and heaven, perhaps the categories no longer matter. More than anything else, what did matter was the impact of such experiences on those who knew them first hand, and who shared them with others who had known comparable experiences. (Cf. David Adam, Living in Two Kingdoms. London, UK: Society for Promoting Christian Knowledge, 2007.)

While revival worship was central to the life of all forms of Methodism, there were also more traditional means of grace that provided food for the journey of all who were making their way in and towards glory. Although the Eucharist was not celebrated as often or as prominently as John Wesley had hoped, it was nevertheless a solemn and life-giving part of quarterly and other meetings, and remained part of the worship experience of Wesley's descendants. Samuel Luckey wrote of Communion in a believer's life, as…

…a constant exhibition of Christ as the spiritual food of the soul, to be received by faith that he may grow thereby; and a renewed assurance of the bestowment of the full grace of the new covenant, in the accomplishment of all its promises, both in this life and that which is to come. In every celebration the *sign* of all these gracious acts, provisions, and hopes is exhibited, and God condescends thus to repeat his *pledges* of faithfulness and love to the Church of Christ, purchased by his blood.

Luckey wondered rhetorically whether "one who has experienced the blessings of pardon and peace through faith in Christ as his Redeemer and Saviour [could] hope to continue in the grace of God, and gain heaven at last," while neglecting this sacrament and ignoring the importance Jesus gave it at the Last Supper. Luckey's book is a clear sign that the importance Wesley gave to Communion as a means of grace, bringing both salvation and sanctification to God's people, strengthening them for the road to glory, had diminished considerably in North American practice. This was not the same world in which Wesley's followers in Britain streamed into parish churches in large numbers to receive the sacramental grace needed for their journey. Yet, at least for some, the Eucharist did function in that original way, providing both a vision of heaven and a resource for attaining it. —Steven David Bruns, *Full Tables, Closed Doors, Open Fields.* Eugene, OR: Pickwick, 2018; Samuel Luckey, including quoted material from Richard Watson, *The Lord's Supper.* New York: Phillips & Hunt; Cincinnati: Walden & Stowe, 1859, 227&229. See also Lorna Khoo, *Wesleyan Eucharistic Spirituality.* Adelaide, AU: ATF, 2005; Daniel B. Stevick, *The Altar's Fire: Charles Wesley's Hymns on the Lord's Supper, 1745 Introduction and Exposition.* Peterborough, UK, 2004.

One of the most unlikely places for joyful worship in the Lord was prison. James Finley sought revival for inmates, warden, and officers, within the walls of the Ohio State Prison in Columbus. Freeborn Garrettson found himself in God's loving presence at a time when he was a victim of persecution. Garrettson had experienced severe persecution, and in this case, "Immediately after escaping an attempt on his life, he was sent by a magistrate to prison." Yet,

> ...during his confinement he was 'much drawn out in prayer, reading, writing and meditation.' ... ...he was 'blessed by the soul-comforting and strengthening letters which he received from pious friends.' 'The Lord,' he says, 'was remarkably good to me, so that I experienced a prison to be like a paradise; and I had a heart to pray for my enemies.' —James B. Finley, *Memorials of Prison Life.* Cincinnati: L. Swormstedt & A. Poe, 1855; Abel Stevens, *Memorials of the Early Progress of Methodism.* Boston: C.H. Peirce, 1852, 87.

Prison was hardly a recommended means of grace, yet for this preacher, that is what it became! It was nothing he volunteered for, but his life with God was so deep and rich that he could say with Joseph, after his own imprisonment, "you meant evil against me, but God meant it for good...." (Genesis 50:20, ESV)

One thing all these experiences of worship had in common was their "Wesleyan emphasis on holiness as the necessary condition for attaining heaven." They started, encouraged, and shepherded people on their road to glory, for they knew "Christian life as a journey or pilgrimage" through an unstable, quickly passing world to an eternity in God's presence. — Lester Ruth, *Early Methodist Life and Spirituality.* Nashville: Kingswood (Abingdon), 2005, 136-138.

Chapter 12

Transition

"Though outwardly we are wasting away, yet inwardly we are being renewed day by day." *II Corinthians 4:16, NIV*

"And take His servants up To their eternal home." —Charles Wesley, "Rejoice, the Lord Is King!" *Hymns of Faith and Life.* Winona Lake, IN: Light and Life Press; Marion, IN: Wesley Press, 1976, #46, v. 4.

When Bishop Edward Andrews spoke at the funeral of Bishop Levi Scott, he quoted Longfellow, saying, "There is no death! What seems so is transition." —quoted in Joseph F. DiPaolo, *Wide Views and a Loving Heart: The Life and Ministry of Bishop Levi Scott.* Philadelphia: Historical Society of the Eastern Pennsylvania Conference of the United Methodist Church, 2018, 104.

Transition experiences fill the pages of circuit rider literature. Resurrection power brought death, "the last enemy," (I Corinthians 15:26, NIV) under God's control, opening up the way to heaven for those who were living in Christ. John Kay wrote that "in his resurrection we see a guarantee of ours. He is the first fruits; He met death on his own domain, conquered him there, robbed him of his power, extracted his sting, disrobed him of his terror, threw open the gates of his prison, and left the monster scathed, enfeebled and prostrate at His feet." Because of the resurrection, for a Christian who is dying, "hope lights up his passage to and through the grave." —John Kay. *Biography of the Rev. William Gundy.* Toronto: James Campbell & Son, 1871, 174.

Whether by age or infirmity; whether sudden or expected, death did not have the last word for these early Methodists. John Lewis Dyer recalled a young family in Wisconsin who had died of cholera, the scourge of their generation. After they were buried, Dyer walked from the grave, "assured that they were safely landed together in the heavenly home. Grace had freed Dyer of his fear of cholera and of death itself, leaving him thankful "to God for his sustaining grace." —John Lewis Dyer, *The Snow-Shoe Itinerant.* Cincinnati: Cranston & Stowe, 1890, 56.

Bishop Levi Scott gave himself fully to his ministry, from his earliest preaching to his episcopacy in the ME Church. He moved his church to fuller acceptance of African American clergy and gave dedicated leadership during the Civil War. He saw sanctification as central to the Christian message and encouraged everyone to seek after it in this life, and as preparation for the next. He worked hard as long as he could, though his steps were slowed by the death of his wife. But when the time came for his own passing, he kept repeating the words, "Come, Lord Jesus, come quickly." His time of service in this world was over, so he was ready to enter another one. —William H. Hutchins, in Joseph F. DiPaolo. *Wide Views and a Loving Heart: The Life and Ministry of Bishop Levi Scott.* Philadelphia: The Historical Society of the Eastern Pennsylvania Conference of The United Methodist Church, 2018, 100.

Old age and the approach of death, when seen from an eternal vantage point, offered to some an opportunity to grow in wisdom, to learn from past experience, and to see life in greater depth. Not everyone is granted this time, but those who walk this road have much to teach us that is of great value.

James Quinn reflected long and deeply on his stage in life, looking back and forward, and articulating the meaning and direction of it all. After a time of "violent pain" and "a dreary season of depression and gloom," a time of relative calm returned and "he soon obtained a comfortable view into the upper sanctuary, as he expressed it, and the cloud bursted (sic), and his soul triumphed in the rock and God of his salvation.…" His friend and biographer, John Wright, "found him happy in the supposed near approach of death, and in the prospect of eternity. While conversing on death and the glory which is to follow his eyes seemed to sparkle with the sacred fires of religion, his soul being inspired by the hope of immortality and eternal life."

Wright recorded many of James Quinn's reflections as death approached, revealing the way he looked back over his life and saw its meaning and direction in light of eternity. There were unexpected days when death withdrew for a time. He "must have realized a most exquisite pleasure in the remembrance of the past. From his point of observation the whole of the checkered scene, through which he had been conducted, appeared spread out before him." For example,

Opportunities of doing good were looked upon as the golden spots of time; and even the toils and sufferings endured, now that they were past, appeared light and momentary, and formed green places along the journey of life. And O, what comfort must the reflection have afforded him, that they would ultimately form a constellation of brilliant stars in the crown of his rejoicing in heaven, when permitted to receive that "exceeding great and eternal weight of glory!"

He recalled people converted along the way, some of them faithful throughout their lives, and others who lost their way. The importance of steadfastness over time grew in his own mind and in these observations of others. Quinn hoped he would have one more opportunity to attend annual conference (1847, in Columbus), and his wish was granted. The Conference asked him for a farewell address, which has been preserved for us. In it he recalled bishops and circuits, events and accomplishments. He painted the broad sweep of time since his early years, peopled by James Finley and Jacob Young, William McKendree and Martin Ruter, along with many others. He concluded,

> Gladly have I spent my all in this work, and long have I endeavored to serve God and his Church. Thank God, I have some fruit of my labor. I have some sons in the Gospel ministry on both sides of the river. I have been connected with you nearly half a century. You see now I am like a reed shaken by the wind, trembling on the brink of the grave. I may never see you all again. O, may we meet in heaven! Let me have an interest in your prayers, that, whether I live or die, I may be wholly the Lord's.

Quinn modified a poem to suit his own reflections, which contrasted youth and age, time and eternity. After recounting his lost or weakening abilities, he writes:

> Days of my age, ye will shortly be passed, Pains of my age, yet awhile may ye last; Joys of my age, in true wisdom delight; Eyes of my age, be religion your light; Thoughts of my age, dread ye not the cold sod; Hopes of my age, be ye fixed on your God. —John F. Wright, *Sketches of the Life and Labors of James Quinn*. Cincinnati: Methodist Book Concern, 1851, 284-301.

To have his hopes "fixed on ... God" was to move beyond self-pity and nostalgia; to see that the grace which has "brought me safe thus far," will also "lead me home." *(John Newton, "Amazing Grace, The United Methodist Hymnal. Nashville: The United Methodist Publishing House, 1989, #378, v. 3.)*

Like James Quinn, David Lewis was afforded time to ponder and reflect on aging and death. Looking back, he said,

> More than forty years of my life have been spent in this work. My pathway has been checkered; the "lights and shades" of itinerancy have alternated in my experience; but, in reviewing the past, I must say, that "goodness and mercy have followed me all the days of my life." Some of the dispensations of Providence have been not only mysterious, but sorely afflictive; yet in the hour of darkness, when earthly comforts fled, and lowering clouds overspread my spiritual sky, I trusted in the Lord, "endured as seeing the invisible," and, through his abounding grace, my soul found refuge and safety.

In another place he looks ahead, guided by imagery from Scripture:

> Most of my family have preceded me to that land which is very far off, where the inhabitants never say they are sick, where all darkness is excluded, where light, pure, unsullied and uninterrupted, reigns forever. There is the absence of all pain, and the presence of all ease – the absence of mortality with its concomitant ills, and the presence of immortality with all its attendant blessings. Blessed world! we may not, while in the flesh, conceive of its unrevealed glories, but, happy for us if, with St. John, we can say, "Beloved, now are we the sons of God, and it doth not yet appear what we shall be: but we know that, when he shall appear, we shall be like him; for we shall see him as he is" This is enough! "We shall be like him;" like the spiritual, immortal, glorified body of Jesus Christ! O what stupendous grace! What boundless love! Let us fall at the feet of Jesus, and adore the God and Rock of our salvation, who hath brought life and immortality to light through the Gospel! Most of my seniors have passed on before me, and many of my juniors have departed this life, while I remain, much like the solitary tree in the open field, exposed to the sweeping blasts of this stormy world; but, unworthy though I be, God is my refuge and defense, my shield and buckler, my high tower and my salvation. His loving-kindness is better than life, and my lips shall praise him. —David Lewis, *Recollections of a Superannuate.* Cincinnati: Methodist Book Concern, 1857, 308-310.

The attitudes they brought into old age were those developed over many years, and they were different from the accustomed attitudes many brought (and still bring) to that time in their lives. Zechariah Paddock draws the contrast between them as he reflects on the aging and death of his brother Benjamin:

> Many people, possibly indeed most, suppose that old men are necessarily peevish, sour, sorrowful, melancholy, or the like. That many old men are so, cannot be denied. The tide of unchanged, unsanctified human nature is doubtless in that direction. And hence the palpable fact that there are aged people who feel nothing but darkness and gloom within themselves, and *see* nothing but darkness and gloom in all that surrounds them. The sources

of sensual enjoyment now all dried up, they see no other sources open to them. The retrospect of the past, the facts of the present, and the anticipations of the future are alike unsatisfactory; so that the spontaneous inquiry is, "Who will show us any good?" – a query not to be solved by any light at their command. No wonder, then, that they are wretched.

This negative, hopeless, complaining attitude contrasts sharply with the character of someone in whom grace has been working for many years. The grim destiny of someone aging and dying without God is not necessary for those who live in Christ.

Such, however, is not the destiny of those who live not unto themselves, but unto Him who died for them and rose again; who have dedicated themselves to God and to humanity; in a word, have practically regarded it as the chief end of their being to glorify God on earth, as well as to enjoy him forever in heaven.

Paddock thought about things he might have done, and was "deeply sorrowful that he had done so little for God and for the salvation of his fellow-men," but took comfort in the efforts he did make, and the grace given him by God. Unlike the gloomy fate of those who have lived selfishly all their lives, he had joy even in weakness, and hope that extended far beyond the confines of this life.

[Paddock] had a smile and a friendly hand for every human being. ... His flesh and his heart might fail, but God was the strength of his heart, and his portion forever. Down to the last moment God was his light and his salvation. The dark valley had no terrors for him. He felt assured that the heavenly Shepherd would not only attend him through it, but lead him to living fountains of water beyond it. He was going home, and rejoiced at the prospect.

As he was dying, "He seized upon the words, Halleluia, for the Lord God omnipotent reigneth," and repeated them again and again with an emphasis and a power that might not inaptly be characterized as unearthly."
—Z. Paddock, *Memoir of Rev. Benjamin G. Paddock,* New York: Nelson & Phillips, 1875, 231-234.

These preachers did not escape the pain and sorrow of aging and death, but those realities never got the last word. Fear and regret did not rule their lives or monopolize their thoughts. Jacob Young is a great example. He once said, "How gloomy and melancholy is old age, unless rendered cheerful by the hope of a better life to come!" These words, noted earlier, reflect a balanced, serious view of old age and its trials. Considering all that had changed in life, and all who had gone, he said, "I am left a lonely wanderer." He had trouble retiring – at age 80! He found it "a dark and trying time." As he came nearer the end, he said, "here I sit, to-day, by the fire-side, a paralytic, eighty years of age, and nearly half blind, yet I am happier than the kings of the earth. Key words here are "unless" and "yet." —Jacob Young, *Autobiography of a Pioneer.* Cincinnati: Cranston & Curts; New York: Hunt & Eaton, n.d., 277; 306; 513; 519.

For Jacob Albright and his friends, the place of dying became also a place to praise God together. Many of his friends assemble at the home of George Becker to surround and support him in his transition. He died among friends who kept watch not in silence, but, at his request, in prayer and song.

> Here he laid himself down to breathe his last. During his illness he enjoyed intimate communion with God.... A number of brethren and sisters who had come to visit him, were deeply affected by his humble prayers of trust, and united with him in his supplications. Soon he achieved a glorious, and, as it proved, his last and eternal victory! He praised God that he was permitted to die surrounded by the people of God, instead of the children of this world, whose only conversation is concerning the affairs of this life. His joy in the Lord was now so great, that he called upon those present to help him praise the Lord. His dying chamber seemed to be the very gate of heaven, and filled with the presence of God. Thus he spent a few days until his last hour on earth approached. George Miller says: He retained the perfect use of his mental faculties to the last. A tranquil mind, which only the consciousness of a well spent life and noble deeds, and the assurance of eternal life and future blessedness can give, could be seen upon his countenance. He bade an affecting and affectionate farewell to those who were present, requesting them to unite with him in praising God, who would soon take his soul unto himself. He gratefully praised his Maker for his providential care over him. And for the guidance of his hand, through which he was led to experience peace and joy, and a living hope through faith in God. ... During the time he bade adieu to his friends with great joy, the house seemed to be filled with the power of God. The children of God felt that heaven was near, and praised God for the manifestation of his power. —R. Yeakel, *Jacob Albright and His Co-Laborers.* Cleveland: Publishing House of the Evangelical Association, 1883, 116&117.

In a similar way, Thomas Morris took his confidence in God's ultimate salvation into his later years, all the way to his last breath:

> I find the religion I so long preached to others is able to bring peace and assurance to the heart in retirement, as well as when in the heat of battle, leading forth the conquering hosts to certain victory. Thank God for the Christian's hope! It comforts and sustains amid all the vicissitudes of life, and to the trusting heart makes bright the future. ... Most of my associates in the ministry, as well as many loved ones, have passed away. I yet

linger on the shores, and soon expect to cross the river. I am nearing the Jordan, and in the course of nature can not stay here much longer; but beneath me are the everlasting arms, and, through riches of grace in Christ Jesus my Lord, I hope to anchor safely in the harbor of eternal rest." ... [His] assurance [was] so strong and comforting, even down to the last moment of his life, that he could say, with his dying breath, "THE FUTURE LOOKS BRIGHT." —John F. Marlay. *The Life of Rev. Thomas A. Morris, D.D.* Cincinnati: Hitchock & Walden; New York: Nelson & Phillips, 1875, 405&406.

AME Bishop William Paul Quinn's last words were recorded and shared in a memorial sermon. Although suffering greatly, he managed to say, after an especially difficult episode, "'Oh, how wonderful is God, how he can uphold us,' and again, 'Another such surge and the war will be over.' 'I am so happy; I see a light brighter than the fire all along my path to heaven.'" The sermon goes on to say that finally,

Though he could not speak, and as the embers of life were slowly losing their force, and as the vital stream was running slow, the premonition of dissolution was seen in the glassy eyes, heard in the rattling throat, or felt in the irregular pulsation , he was still conscious though not able to speak. Like some brave warrior, who, surrounded with the smoke of battle, is seen waving the battle flag, he would look up with a smile, and wave his hand in triumph over the last enemy. He waved and waved, like friends parting, until he had passed out of the world and the church. – *In Memoriam: Funeral Services in Respect to the Memory of Rev. William Paul Quinn.* Toledo: Warren Chapel, 1873, 25&26.

Thomas Stockton was known both for his eloquence and "his humility of spirit." As his biographer noted, "Popularity is dangerous to any man – is the ruin of many a man. To be complimented, to be lauded, to be followed by adoring throngs, is what few can endure without injury. But it has always been evident that Stockton cared not for the honor that cometh from men."

Stockton's reputation as a "pulpit orator" is borne out in his dying words:

I trust I am going to see the grandest thing in the universe: the light of the knowledge of God in the face of Christ Jesus our Lord.

I can not tell you how happy I am, at the prospect of getting at the center of universal intelligence, through the mercy of God in Christ Jesus our Lord.
—Ancel H. Bassett, *A Concise History of the Methodist Protestant Church.* Pittsburgh: James Robison; Baltimore: W.J.C. Dulaney, 1882, 423; 422.

Jacob Gruber related an amazing story that accentuates how close the connection between camp meeting worship and heaven could be: "Another lady who was in declining health desired to be taken to the camp ground that she might go to heaven from that spot. She was accordingly taken, and 'in transports of joy she went up to join the song of the redeemed.'" —W.P. Strickland, *The Life of Jacob Gruber.* New York: Carlton & Porter, 1860, 43.

Wyandotte Chief Rhon-Yan-Ness, once an enemy of Christianity, experienced a powerful reconciliation with Methodist preacher Adam Poe, which led to the chief's conversion. While not a licensed or ordained minister, Rhon-Yan-Ness became a class leader and major influence within his nation. James Finley said of Rhon-Yan-Ness, "His whole life was unblamable, and his character as a Christian irreproachable; and we never knew a Christian in any nation, or among any people, more innocent, guileless, and happy than Rhon-Yan-Ness. Rooted and grounded in love he was steadfast in his profession...." Rhon-Yan-Ness died shortly after speaking at a quarterly meeting. At the love feast, he shared his experience of coming to Christ. "Raising his eyes toward heaven, he clapped his hands, and shouted in prospect of his long-sought home." —W.P. Strickland, ed., *James Finley, Sketches of Western Methodism.* Cincinnati: Methodist Book Concern, 1855, 549-551.

Nathan Emery "was disposed to look upon death with some degree of dread, and to speak of the last conflict with the 'grim monster;' and as he saw the hour of dissolution approaching, he nerved himself for the dying strife. He sought earnestly for dying grace, and that grace in rich abundance was given." Since it is natural for most of us to "look upon death with some degree of dread," we can both identify with brother Emery, and rejoice in the gift of "dying grace." Emery "realized that the God of Abraham, Isaac, and Jacob was with him, and all was well." Not only was he able to say goodbye to his daughter and friends, with "many precious words of comfort and consolation," but he was also given visions of things to come. Like many others documented in that early period, Emery described to those around him the first moments of his transition to a new life.

> Visions of glory ... were reserved for this dying herald of the cross, such as he had never witnessed before. As he neared the Jordan, and the land of Beulah spread out its bowers on either hand, ...he was enabled to see the celestial city on the other shore, while he was fanned by its breezes, regaled by its odors, and enraptured by its transporting sounds. When his pilgrim feet touched the dark, cold waters, he exclaimed, "O, how gently my Savior leads me through!" —W.P. Strickland, ed., *James B. Finley,*

Sketches of Western Methodism. Cincinnati: Methodist Book Concern, 1855, 337&338.

Thomas Whitehead's transition was very evident to those who watched with him. John Carroll describes what they witnessed;

> He preached for the last time in his life on Christmas day, 1845, from Luke ii. 14. While his body, literally worn out, was gradually sinking beneath the accumulation of years and labours, the vigour of his intellect remained unimpaired – his peace perfect – his hope buoyant. His eye of luminous faith converted the darkness of death into the opening light of Heaven, and transformed its gloomy valley into a highway of triumph; and while he was giving the sign of assured victory, after speech had failed, he fell asleep in Jesus, having furnished practical commentary during a longer period than any other Clergyman in Canada.... —John Carroll, *Past and Present.* Toronto: Alfred Dredge, 1860, 77&78.

Early Methodists reflected on death and eternity in some of the hymns they wrote. James O'Kelly, known as a leader of the first breakaway denomination, the Republican Methodist Church, said in one of his hymns, "Death is the gate to endless pleasure, the road to everlasting joy." In another place he looked forward to a time when those who made their way into heaven would be "Free'd from sickness, free'd from sorrow, free'd from anguish care and pain." Linking sanctification with eternity, he wrote, "I long to see thy glorious face, And in thine image shine; to triumph in thy glorious grace, And be forever thine." Kelly drew from Revelation 21 to say that in God's heaven, "No night is there, but endless day, New glories constant rise; The loving LAMB shall wipe away The tears from all their eyes." This theme stands out as especially important in O'Kelly's collection. —James O'Kelly, *Hymns and Spiritual Songs.* London, UK: Forgotten Books, 2015, Songs, pp. 11 & 29; Hymns, p. 3

Far from ignoring death or the painful realities of this life, preachers and hymn writers frequently contrasted this world's trials and transience with liberation and joy in heaven, "Where endless pleasures banish pain." —William Colbert, *poem on the death of a young woman called Grace Griffith, in Lester Ruth, Early Methodist Life and Spirituality: A Reader. Nashville: Abingdon, 2005, 292.* United Brethren circuit rider J.K. Alwood wrote the hopeful hymn, "O They Tell Me of a Home," including this chorus: "O that land of cloudless day, O the land of an unclouded day; O they tell me of a home where no storm clouds rise, O they tell me of an unclouded day." And Samuel Y. Harmer, another Methodist preacher, called Christians to,

> Sing. O sing ye heirs of glory!

> Shout your triumph as you go!
> Zion's gate will open for you,
> You shall find an entrance through. —Samuel Y. Harmer, *"In the Christian's Home in Glory," in African Methodist Episcopal Church Hymnal.* Nashville: AMEC, 1984, #504, v. 3.

Maxwell Gaddis published a large collection of *Last Words and Old Time Memories* that captured something of the experience of preachers transitioning from this life to the next. When I opened that book, I expected it to be somewhat depressing. It is not. In fact, it is positively inspiring. He also gathered accounts of the dying experiences of ministers' wives, in which these words form part of the introduction:

> ...we may have the pivotal point of being so energized by the Holy Ghost that all things turn toward God in us, we may so have our conversation in heaven that the law of spiritual gravity would carry us to the foot of the throne, but as far as our mental and bodily life is concerned, we are still subject to the devastating influences of the fall, and we groan and wait, and are saved by hope.... —Mrs. E.T. Wells, Introduction to Maxwell Pierson Gaddis, *Saintly Women and Death-Bed Triumphs.* http.//www.JawboneDigital.com, 2015 (original, 1880).

Gaddis published several books, including an autobiography and biographical works on other Methodist preachers. His collection of last or dying words of hundreds of circuit riders gives us an amazing view of their transition to a life they had already glimpsed from time to time across their careers. It includes final messages to family, friends, and colleagues, along with confirmation of the faith they had preached and lived all their lives. It also allows us to witness a portion of their forward movement from this life to the next.

One powerful example is that of Daniel Edgerton, who at age twenty-seven was making his way to heaven. "Several weeks before his death, in a class meeting, he said,"

> I stand on the platform, waiting for the heavenly train, - satchel in one hand and ticket in the other. I know it will take me through, for it is stamped with the blood of Jesus. I know I am going to live. Heaven seems so much brighter and real than ever before; and the plan of salvation so clear. It is like starting on a journey. You see the city in the distance; then nearer, until it is in full view. So it is with heaven, grand and glorious. Do not weep when I am gone. Sing the doxology. Angels! Angels! Sing "Praise God from whom all blessings flow." —Maxwell Pierson Gaddis, *Last Words and Old Time Memories.* New York & Pittsburgh: Phillips & Hunt; Cincinnati & Chicago: Walden & Stowe, 1880, 83.

Gaddis says of G.W. Harris, another young preacher, that "During his last hours he gave his friends all the evidence they could ask that he was ready for his change – from earth to glory." Another preacher, Harvey Husted, passed a portion of his last hours singing,

> My latest sun is sinking fast,
> My race is nearly run;
> My strongest trials now are past,
> My triumph is begun. —Maxwell Pierson Gaddis, *Last Words and Old-Time Memories (etc.)*. New York & Pittsburgh: Phillips & Hunt; Cincinnati & Chicago: Walden & Stowe, 1880, 131 & 135.

Over the days when Methodist Protestant pastor Hannah Reeves was dying, she testified to having "long overcome both the *fear of death* and of *dying*! At one point she felt herself "quite on the verge of heaven," and later said, "Blessed Jesus! He is with me, and I knew he would be with me to the end. He told me he would, and he is with me now. ... Hallelujah! Hallelujah! Glory! Glory! Glory!" Still later, she said, "Let me go, let me go for I want to go and see the God I love." She recited lines from Augustus Toplady's "When Languor and Disease Invade," which were highly appropriate to her situation. Among its verses are these:

> When languor and disease invade
> This trembling house of clay,
> 'Tis sweet to look beyond my pains,
> And long to fly away.
>
> Sweet to look back and see my name
> In life's fair book set down;
> Sweet to look forward and behold
> Eternal joys my own. —George Brown, *The Lady Preacher, or, The Life and Labor of Mrs. Hannah Reeves*. Philadelphia: Daughaday & Becker; Springfield, OH: Methodist Publishing House, 1870, 313-316; Augustus Toplady, *"When Languor and Disease Invade,"* Hymnary.Org.

Wesley C. Hudson died in New Brunswick, after ten years of youthful ministry. "Just before he departed he said to his wife, 'I am going home to glory, my love, and shall look for you daily.' When he came to the moment of his departure, he said 'I am stepping over Jordan [the Jordan River, a commonly used image for the transition from earthly life to eternity].'" Joseph Newson was "asked if the religion he had preached to others sustained him now, [to which] he replied with emphasis, 'I have not followed a cunningly-devised fable. I have looked over the road to the grave many a time, and now it is not dark. It's all light. Not a cloud hovers over my spiritual horizon. All is bright!'"

Conrad Pluenneke's remarkable Texas ministry came to an end in 1897. Before he passed, he used part of his time to remember all that had happened during his life, wondering "What had enabled him to do all those things." He remembered that "it was the finger of God that quietly showed me the way at each crucial step of my life." Near the end of his life, he whispered aloud, "Tonight I will be with God" and smiled that faint smile for which he was known. At midday, he smiled broadly at a vision of a crooked finger beckoning him. Summoning the rest of his energy, he said a loud Amen to the vision that only he could see and followed that with "Lord, I will come." – Robert Lamar Feuge, *The Life and Times of a German Methodist Circuit Rider on the Frontier of Texas.* n.c.: n.p., 2014, 326.

As Bishop George was approaching death, he said, "Rejoice with me, I am going to glory. I have been many years trying to lead others to glory, and now thither I am going." —W.P. Strickland, *The Life of Jacob Gruber.* New York: Carlton & Porter, 1860, 36&37.

Like many others, Andrew Craig Field turned to send words of wisdom to his colleagues, "Tell the preachers I am going through the gates into the city trusting in Jesus." These words followed those shared with his doctor: "I am going where Christ is. ... As I near the shore I feel increasing attraction. —Maxwell Pierson Gaddis, *Last Words and Old Time Memories (etc.).* New York & Pittsburgh: Phillips & Hunt; Cincinnati & Chicago: Walden & Stowe, 1880, 131, 135, 159, 227 & 91.

These and countless others testify to a departure from this life that was also an entrance to the life to come. Nothing in that transition took away the pain or sickness, the separation from loved ones, or the end of a ministry. Instead, it fulfilled their calling, purpose, and discipleship. It confirmed the message they had spread far and wide, and it served as a milestone in their transfiguration. The vision that had propelled them forward, renewed in times of intense prayer, worship, and fellowship, was beginning to be their immediate reality. We can be enormously thankful that so many, with the help of friends and colleagues, spent their last days and moments sharing that reality with us.

Davis W. Clark contributed a volume of *Death-Bed Scenes*, spanning the centuries but including examples from American Methodism. His purpose was to demonstrate the difference in experience between those who approached death with or without Christian faith. Among them was a comment from Wilbur Fisk, comparing Sundays with heaven's peace. "To me the Sabbath has always been an emblem of that promised rest. O, that rest is sweet! It is glorious!" To his wife, he said, "Think not, when you see this poor feeble body stretched in death, that this is your husband. O no! your husband will have escaped, free and liberated.... Of his spiritual, heavenly body he said, "It will be perfect, for it will be fashioned like unto Christ's most glorious body, and united with the soul forever!" S.B. Bangs ended his life saying, "Not a doubt, not a cloud. All well – more than well. Praise the Lord, I am going home." Then, after singing a hymn, he said, "The sun ... is setting, mine is rising." In another case, as he was dying, William Romaine, said,

> I have the peace of God in my conscience, and the love of God in my heart. I knew before the doctrines I preached to be truths, but now I experience them to be blessings. Jesus is more precious than rubies, and all that can be desired on the earth is not to be compared with him. ... Holy, holy, holy, Lord God Almighty! Glory be to thee on high, for such peace on earth, and good-will to men. —Davis W. Clark, *Death-Bed Scenes*. New-York: Carlton & Porter, 1851, 208&209; 212; 257.

Another moving story comes from the transition experience of Henry Culp, who passed in 1882:

> "I have prayed that the veil might be lifted before I crossed over, and it is. My spiritual sky is as clear as the noonday sun. I see the open gates of the New Jerusalem, the river and the trees of life, and I am going to live with my heavenly Father." For an hour he seemed to see and describe the beauty of the Heavenly City. He then said: "I have tried to preach Christ in life, and now I can say, 'Behold! behold! the Lamb!' We never heard a more vivid description of heaven than came from his lips." —*Minutes of the Ohio Conference ... of the Methodist Episcopal Church, 1883*. Cincinnati: Western Methodist Book Concern, 1883, 62.

Such experiences were far from restricted to ministers. Dr. T.W. Cowgill, a medical professor at Indiana Asbury University, as he was dying, spoke of "limitless, unbounded joy – it was full redemption." Clark tells us that "To those who were with him it seemed as though the room had been filled with the glory of God, and they were strongly reminded of the scene of the Pentecost." At one point he said, "I have been ... able to look upon death before with composure; but never before could I look clear through the dark and gloomy vault, quite up into heaven. O, such a fullness, such an infinity of joy!" Nor were these incidents confined demographically. Clark relates the dying experience of Agnes Morris, an extremely poor slave on the island of Antigua. A Methodist teacher found her lying on "a board, with a few plantain-leaves over it." After singing some hymns, Agnes "was in a rapture of joy," and she took the time to ask the teacher to "'show um de pa,' – meaning the path to heaven. Many other expressions fell from her of a similar nature, to the astonishment of those who heard her." Clark ended the account by asking "How many of these outcasts will be translated from outward wretchedness to realms of glory!" —Davis W. Clark, *Death-Bed Scenes*. New-York: Carlton & Porter, 1851, 315&316; 392.

While today many people seem to accept this life as "all there is," such acceptance was far from the consciousness of early Methodist preachers. Committed though they were to making a difference in this world, they knew there was something better awaiting them in the next. In a hymn, part of which appeared in a United Brethren hymnal, Charles Giles recognized the transience of this world, starkly contrasting with God's eternal kingdom:

> This world is poor, from shore to shore,
> And, like a baseless vision,
> Its lofty domes and brilliant ore,
> Its gems and crowns, are vain and poor;
> There's nothing rich but heaven.
>
> Fine gold will change, and diamonds fade,
> Swift wings to wealth are given;
> All varying time our forms invade -
> The seasons roll, light sinks in shade;
> There's nothing lasts but heaven.
>
> Empires decay and nations die,
> Our hopes to wind are given;
> The vernal blooms in ruin lie,
> Death reigns o'er all beneath the sky:
> There's nothing sure but heaven.
>
> Creation's mighty fabric all
> Shall be to atoms riven, -
> The skies consume, the planets fall,
> Convulsions rock this earthly ball;
> There's nothing firm but heaven.
>
> A stranger, lonely here I roam,
> From place to place am driven;
> My friends are gone, and I'm in gloom,
> This earth is all a dismal tomb;
> I have no home but heaven.

And finally, in words appropriate for one who has lived, served, and grown in this world and is ready to enter the next, we hear echoes of countless transition experiences:

> The clouds disperse, the light appears
> My sins are all forgiven;
> Triumphant grace has quelled my fears
> Roll on, thou Sun, fly swift my years,
> I'm on my way to heaven. —Charles Giles, *"This World Is Poor from Shore to Shore,"* found at Hymnary.org.

How is it that so many could face the hour of death with courage and confidence? What enabled them to see the road to glory going on ahead of them, even as they said goodbye to loved ones on this part of their journey? Benjamin Abbott attended a funeral at which the minister said that, "Death was the king of terrors, and that he made cowards of us all."

> After sermon, Mr. Abbott took an opportunity to converse with Mr. S. (who had said those words) on the subject, and said that he did not believe the doctrine: for "perfect love casteth out fear, and he that feareth is not made perfect in love;" and that he believed a state attainable in this life, through grace, that would enable us to shout victory to God and the Lamb, "through the valley of the shadow of death;" nay, through death itself, and "fear no evil." Also, that he had seen many leave this world in the greatest transport of joy imaginable; and in one or two instances, that he did believe they had seen the angels of God with their bodily eyes, before their departure. "And for my part," said he, "I can call God to witness, that death is no terror to me! I am ready to meet my God, if it were now!" —John Ffirth, *Experience and Gospel Labors of Benjamin Abbott: To which is Annexed a Narrative of His Life and Death.* New-York: J. Emory & B. Waugh, 1830, 202&203; For more examples of such visions, Cf. Lester Ruth, *Early Methodist Life and Spirituality.* Nashville: Kingswood (Abingdon), 2005, 146-152.

As these preachers came to the end of this life, they were often surrounded by family and personal friends, but also by colleagues whose appointments or travels placed them in a position to pay a visit. The conversations they shared can be very instructive. For Orange Scott, who had left the Methodist Episcopal Church with others to form the Wesleyan Methodist Connexion, there was time for his Wesleyan colleagues to pray with him. He also mentioned another caller, whose visit was much appreciated: "Brother Wakeley, pastor of the M.E. Church, has called and prayed with me twice. This was very kind of him, and I am grateful for it." In reply, a friend "told him of the kind notice Brother Stevens took of his sickness in the Herald, and the expressions of others toward him, of sympathy and kind regard." —Lucius C. Matlack, *The Life of Rev. Orange Scott.* New York: C. Prindle & L.C. Matlack, 1847, 277. Joseph Beaumont Wakeley and Abel Stevens were prominent biographers and historians within the Methodist Episcopal Church.

Such expressions of Christian fellowship, transcending conflicts that had divided them from one another, reflect a deeper connection that embraces our entire tradition, and the faith of which it is a part. That is not to say that the issues they stood for or the vision of the church they advanced were unimportant. Yet while, like all of us, Orange Scott had sung, "What troubles have we seen, What mighty conflicts past," yet there must be a time – surely the transition from life's end to heaven's beginning is one of them – when we must put troubles and conflicts behind us, "and gladly reckon all things loss so we may Jesus gain." —Charles Wesley, *"And Are We Yet Alive,"* in The United Methodist Hymnal. Nashville: United Methodist Publishing House, 1989, #553, vs. 3&6.

CHAPTER 13

Direction

"Lead me in the way everlasting." —*Psalm 139:24, NIV*

"And still to things eternal look, And hasten to thy glorious day." —Charles Wesley, "Forth in Thy Name," *The Hymnal.* Harrisburg & Dayton: Board of Publication of The Evangelical United Brethren Church, 1957, #35, v.3.

Among those who faced the most severe frontier conditions was John Lewis Dyer as he ministered in, and traveled between, the mining towns of Colorado. One incident illustrates both his determination to live and serve in this world, and his assurance of another world to come:

> …I was met by a severe snow-storm. Had a box of matches, but not one would burn. The prospect was frightful. I prayed and dedicated myself to God, and thought by his grace I would try to pull through. For five or six hours I waded in the snow waist-deep, until, almost exhausted, I leaned up against a tree to rest. I never saw death and eternity so near as then. My life seemed to be at an end,; but I resolved to keep moving, and when I could go no more, would hang up my carpet-sack, and write on a smooth pine-tree my own epitaph – "Look for me in heaven;" but through the goodness of God, I reached the toll-gate about one hour after dark; and I shall never forget the kindness of the Swede who took me in and cared for me. —John Lewis Dyer, *The Snow-Shoe Itinerant.* Cincinnati: Cranston & Stowe, 1890, 136.

Dyer was typical of circuit riders who acknowledged and depended upon God's grace to accomplish daunting tasks, prepared either to live "through the goodness of God," or to make their way into heaven by that same grace. There was no contest here between pursuing their mission or focusing on "things above." (Colossians 3:2, NIV) They took seriously their commission as witnesses for Christ, even as they "press[ed] on …

heavenward in Christ Jesus." (Philippians 3:14, NIV) They lived out of the perspective of eternity, and from that perspective worked tirelessly for the expansion of eternity's kingdom. Even as their life was "now hidden with Christ in God," they poured themselves out in order "to serve the present age." Such was the paradox of an eternity that was both present and future. Heaven could lift them above hardship while moving them through it. For them it was both goal and motivation. —Colossians 3:3, NIV; Charles Wesley, *"A Charge to Keep I Have," The African Methodist Episcopal Church Hymnal.* Nashville: AMEC, #242, v.2.

In his book on Christian perfection, George Peck made the necessary connection between heaven and holiness. Most of his book details both the mandate and blessings of Christian perfection in the context of this life – on this world and its people, on preachers and converts, and on the influence of Christ toward the world's transformation. But he also sees it as preparation for eternity, where sin is unwelcome and human destiny is to be fully lived out.

> But how does the importance of the attainment [of Christian perfection] increase when we look to the final hour? When called to contend with the swellings of Jordan, of what inconceivable importance will it be to us to be in a state of entire readiness to pass into our changeless state! —George Peck. *The Scripture Doctrine of Christian Perfection.* New-York: Carlton & Phillips, 1854, 430.

The point of growing in Christ, of sanctification and a new creation within ourselves, is *permanent* transformation, resulting in a change of character in this life that makes a difference in the world *and* propels us into eternity. Imagine a scenario in which our growth in grace would be for this life only. Where would be the power of the resurrection that Jesus shares with us? What would be our eventual fate if we had nothing to look forward to? What would happen to the depth of prayer and worship if there were no heaven to break into our midst in a blaze of glory and carry us home to the fulfillment of that glory? We would have to say, with Paul, "If only for this life we have hope in Christ, we are of all people most to be pitied." (I Corinthians 15: 19, NIV) But the promise comes from Jesus himself: "Because I live, you also will live." (John 14:19, NIV) He prepares a place for us in heaven, even as he has prepared "a table" for us here. (John 14:2&3; Psalm 23:5, NIV) His resurrection achieves its purpose in our own. His shares his destiny with us, so that, audacious as it sounds, "…we shall be like him…." (I John 3:2, NIV) Sanctifying grace leads us to and prepares us for eternity with him. It is by the power of the Spirit that we are "being transformed into his image with ever-increasing glory...." (II Corinthians 3:18, NIV) Finally we will live with him in "a new heaven and a new earth." (Revelation 21:1, NIV; Cf. Isaiah 65:17)

Eventually the Methodist movement changed in a variety of ways that weakened and diluted its life and witness, something that at least some of its own leaders recognized as it was happening. David Kimbrough writes that "Methodism lost its communal and spiritual character as cultural alienation gave way to a pilgrimage to respectability." The churches which changed the most were the Methodist Episcopal Church and the Methodist Church of Canada, but similar changes would eventually come to others. —David L. Kimbrough, *Reverend Joseph Tarkington, Methodist Circuit Rider: From Frontier Evangelism to Refined Religion.* Knoxville: University of Tennessee Press, 1997, xiv. Cf. Kevin Watson, *Old School or New School Methodism?: The Fragmentation of a Theological Tradition.* New York: Oxford University Press, 2019.

As the nineteenth century wore on, some Methodist preachers and writers had to argue with great energy to maintain the practices and underlying theology that had always characterized the Wesleyan movement. Class meetings and camp meetings; quarterly meetings and even circuits themselves, faded or lost their original character until they no longer served the same purposes, at least not in the same way or with the same results. While there remained significant differences among Methodist denominations and regional practices, especially in the Wesleyan Holiness Movement, there was a general move from red hot evangelism to more sedate forms of appropriating the faith. The simplicity of our early church buildings yielded to an insatiable desire for expensive and impressive facilities that resembled those of established churches in Europe. Congregational singing remained important, but there were also choirs, pipe organs, and more sophisticated musical offerings. Many churches became gathering places for the affluent, powerful, and well educated, leaving the poor to find their own way. Self-education and solid but increasingly dated theological literature made way for universities, seminaries, and trans-oceanic, trans-denominational theological movements. Trends in secular universities attracted debate and sometimes acceptance in colleges of the Methodist churches. The high intensity, life transforming spirituality of the old revivals became increasingly sublimated to well organized educational and cultural activities, perhaps symbolized best by the Chautauqua Institution and its imitators and outreach to cities and even rural communities. Methodist academics struggled to relate Biblical theology to new waves of secular thought. —John H. Vincent, *The Chautauqua Movement.* Boston: Chautauqua Press, 1886, and also his *The Revival and After the Revival.* New York: Phillips & Hunt; Cincinnati: Cranston & Stowe, 1882; *The*

Ingham Lectures ... Ohio Wesleyan University. Cleveland: Ingham, Clarke & Company; Cincinnati: Hitchcock & Walden; New York: Nelson & Phillips, 1872.

Peter Cartwright, along with many others, commented on this pattern:

> Look at the needless, not to say sinful expenditures in our older cities and districts of the country; the unnecessary thousands expended, not in building needful and decent churches, for this is right, but ornamental churches, to make a vain show and gratify pampered pride. Look at the ornamented pulpits, pewed and cushioned seats, organs, and almost all kinds of instruments, with salaried choirs, and as proud and graceless as a fallen ghost, while millions upon millions of our fallen race are dying daily, and peopling the regions of eternal woe for want of the Gospel of Jesus Christ; and as scarce as ministers are in some places in our own happy country, yet there are thousands that are ready and willing to go to the utmost verge of this green earth, and carry the glad tidings of mercy to those dying millions, if they had the means of support. —W.P. Strickland, ed. *Autobiography of Peter Cartwright.* New York: Phillips & Hunt; Cincinnati: Walden & Stowe, 1856, 235.

James V. Watson recalled the original quarterly meetings with great admiration and nostalgia. He saw that their time had passed, but hoped that "something equally good and useful: might take their place." In that hope, we can see one aspect of a much needed direction. "Alas! the old-fashioned quarterly meeting is henceforth to be but a thing of history. But if we cannot restore it, can we not substitute something equally good and useful?" —James V. Watson, *Tales and Takings, Sketches and Incidents.* New-York: Carlton & Porter, 1856, 373.

Canadian Methodists followed similar patterns in affluence, theology, practices, and organization, until Wesleyan distinctives were largely lost in the 1925 merger that created The United Church of Canada. The Free Methodists would see themselves as "a remnant that would preserve the message and heritage" of Methodism in Canada, and would be joined by Wesleyans, The Salvation Army, and much later a large, independent congregation called the Toronto Chinese Methodist Church. One Free Methodist historian asked concerning the modernized Methodism that joined in the merger: "Was there any reason for the continued existence of a denomination that no longer adhered to its own founding principles?" —See Neil Semple, *The Lord's Dominion: The History of Canadian Methodism.* Montreal & Kingston; London, UK & Buffalo: McGill-Queens University Press, 1996; R. Wayne Kleinsteuber, *More than a Memory: The Renewal of Methodism in Canada.* n.c.: Light and Life Press Canada, 1984, 79; 66.

David Hempton has shown how the deterioration of anti-slavery in the American Methodist mainstream coincided with early signs of decline in growth, obscured by the obvious success of the churches across the century. In his autobiography, Peter Cartwright noted both the split between northern and southern Methodists (M.E. & M.E., S.), and the breaking away of Wesleyans and others representing abolitionism. He rightly saw this pattern of division as prefiguring the division of the nation. —David Hempton, *Methodism: Empire of the Spirit.* New Haven, CT and London, UK: Yale University Press, 2005; W.P. Strickland, ed., *Autobiography of Peter Cartwright.* New York: Carlton & Porter, 1854, 128&129; 414-424; 437-440.

African American churches have needed to devote enormous energy to the causes of liberation from slavery and achieving genuine equality in all aspects of American society. They have worked hard to live their Wesleyan character as they implement Wesley's commitment to justice and freedom. —See, for example, William J. Walls, *The African Methodist Episcopal Zion Church.* Charlotte: A.M.E. Zion Publishing House, 1974, 29-34; Richard S. Newman, *Freedom's Prophet: Bishop Richard Allen, the AME Church, and the Black Founding Fathers;* Douglas F. Powe, *Just Us or Justice? Moving Toward a Pan-Methodist Theology.* Nashville: Abingdon, 2009.

Yet the Wesleyan evangelical movement has also shown great resilience. From it, both inside and out of its organized denominations, has come the Holiness revival, and then the Pentecostal movement, which has swept across the globe and brought new vitality to Christian life in Pentecostal, independent, and mainstream churches. Within Methodist denominations there is considerable interest in exploring our heritage and re-engaging with its pioneers and all they can teach us. In mainstream denominations there is considerable unrest among those who see the distance between much of what happens in church life today and the original purpose that once animated our churches. In The United Methodist Church, for example, heir to the Methodist Episcopal, Methodist Episcopal, South, Methodist Protestant, Evangelical, and United Brethren expressions of our faith, there is a growing movement seeking to break out of the pattern of decline by establishing a new church that would build on the Scriptural, traditional foundation of original Methodism. In other denominations and parts of the world, there are efforts to reinvigorate church life through more effective evangelism and multicultural ministry. Still others continue to pursue freedom, equality, and justice in church and society. Churches that began with a strong commitment to anti-slavery are now working to free victims of modern human trafficking. Immigrant communities are bringing the vitality of their home churches as an example of what North American churches once were, and could again become.

This book has focused, however, on one particular aspect of life and ministry: our beliefs and experiences related to the temporary realities of this life and the eternal reality that is both coextensive with, transcends, and survives those temporary realities. Eternity shapes our identity, our self-perceptions, and the meaning we find in life, death, and resurrection. Eternity allows us to see all that goes on in this world from God's perspective, beyond time and human limitations. Rootedness in eternity means that those who forged our North American Wesleyan identity can still teach all of us who happen to be living in a very different generation.

When Dan Young (in 1860) wanted to share what was most important for a new generation, he focused on eternity. His words speak as clearly today as they did in his own time:

> How immeasurably important is everything which pertains to an eternal state of existence! If you would make an estimate of the number of minutes which you may live on earth, and then to each minute apply a million ages, it is only the vestibule, just the beginning of that future state of existence which shall never, never close! And are we not insane to remain indifferent and unconcerned whether we are prepared or not for such a state? —W.P. Strickland, *Autobiography of Dan Young*. New York: Carlton & Porter, 1860, 365&366.

Yet in recent years, the churches in our movement have focused so heavily on everyday realities of this world, that we have lost the clarity we once had concerning eternal life and the eternal dimensions of this life. Far from being "so heavenly minded we're no earthly good," we have succeeded in reversing that expression. Our effectiveness in ministry declines as we lose sight of, and resources from, God's eternal kingdom. We have long lived in a condition where we cannot even approach or imagine the impact our ancestors made on the society of their time. We must come to see ourselves once again, across time and space, as pilgrims together on the road to glory.

This means that we must fully recover, and commit ourselves to, genuine, orthodox theology. We must see our spiritual growth as heading toward an infinite destiny. We must seek transformation that is far beyond anything we can accomplish apart from the outpouring of the Holy Spirit. We must see each other, those close to us, and those far away, as equal, cherished companions on this journey. We must live from an eternal perspective, so that we prioritize our lives according to what really matters. We must resist and refuse the temptation to jettison our Christian, Wesleyan past for an empty, secular, hedonistic future. We will need resources for all this, many of the same resources our Methodist ancestors enjoyed – the means of grace.

We need each other, together in congregations that worship in ways that break through conventionality, reaching back into our past and build a future that is open to, and led by, the transforming power of God. We need accountability and encouragement, so that something like class meetings can be an integral part of our Christian life and relationships. We need a vision of heaven that inspires and empowers us to seek that kingdom above all else, and to work as we pray that God's will is done "on earth as it is in heaven" – through us. In doing this, we must not idolize any purely political, human-made ideology or movement. We cannot confuse any organization or nation or cause with the kingdom. But we must also do what we can to shine the light of Christ around us, so that the world will come to live by that light. With the Irish Christian band Rend Collective, we need to plead with God to "Build Your Kingdom Here."

To achieve this outrageously ambitious agenda will only be possible, as with everything else that is part of our sanctification, by grace, with our willing, energized cooperation. We will need to reopen channels of communication among the denominations of our Methodist family, and deepen our awareness of what our tradition offers to all Christians, and to the world. The task is surely beyond us, but not beyond God. When we look at our early history, we realize what can happen when God and his people work in divinely initiated synergy.

CHAPTER 14

Peculiarities

"Now we are all here in the presence of God to listen to everything the Lord has commanded you to tell us." —*Acts 10:33, NIV*

"O Thou who camest from above, the pure celestial fire t'impart, kindle a flame of sacred love on the mean altar of my heart." —Charles Wesley, "O Thou Who Camest From Above," *The A.M.E. Zion Hymnal.* Charlotte: A.M.E. Zion Publishing House, 1957, #375, v. 1.

Transformation often took place at camp meetings and continued in local services, class meetings, spiritual reading and personal devotions. At camp meetings there were sometimes examples of what even then came across as bizarre behavior, which in spite of its strangeness could produce change, by literally shaking people out of their complacency or hostility, let alone their expectations of suitable behavior. Hard as it may be for us to relate to such things, or take them seriously, impossible as it may be to transfer them to another time and place, we cannot ignore the impact of such phenomena on people of that early time. This strange and moving behavior took several forms. Here is a description of one of them - "the jerks" - in the writing of Peter Cartwright:

> Just in the midst of our controversies on the subject of the powerful exercises among the people under preaching, a new exercise broke out among us, called the *jerks*, which was overwhelming in its effects upon the bodies and minds of the people. No matter whether they were saints or sinners, they would be taken under a warm song or sermon, and seized with a convulsive jerking all over, which they could not by any possibility avoid, and the more they resisted the more they jerked. If they would not strive against it and [would] pray in good earnest, the jerking would usually abate. I have seen more than five hundred persons jerking at one time in my large congregations. Most usually persons taken with the jerks, to

obtain relief, would rise up and dance. Some would run, but could not get away. Some would resist; on such the jerks were generally very severe.

To see those proud young gentlemen and young ladies, dressed in their silks, jewelry, and prunella ["A smooth woolen stuff, generally black, used for making shoes or garments"], from top to toe, take the jerks, would often excite my risibilities ["Proneness to laugh"]. The first jerk or so, you would see their fine bonnets, caps, and combs fly; and so sudden would be the jerking of the head that their long loose hair would crack almost as loud as a wagoner's whip. —W.P. Strickland, ed., *Autobiography of Peter Cartwright, The Backwoods Preacher.* New York: Phillips & Hunt; Cincinnati: Walden & Stowe, 1856, 48&49; Noah Webster, *An American Dictionary of the English Language.* Springfield, MA: George & Charles Merriam, 1848, 885; 959.

This was not the first time "the jerks" made their appearance in revival meetings, often accompanied by "falling," or being "slain," a spiritual state resembling unconsciousness or sleep. William Henry Milburn describes the scene at Cane Ridge, the first of all camp meetings and one which involved more than Methodists. The particular instance he cites happened as Methodist circuit rider William Burke was preaching in a kind of impromptu gathering on the grounds:

It is said that all these people, the whole ten thousand of men and women standing about the preacher, were from time to time shaken as a forest by a tornado, and five hundred were at once prostrated to the earth, like the trees in a "windfall," by some invisible agency. Some were agitated by violent whirling motions, some by fearful contortions; and then came "the jerks." Scoffers, doubters, deniers, men who came to ridicule and sneer at the supernatural agency, were taken up in the air, whirled over upon their heads, coiled up so as to spin about like cart-wheels, catching hold, meantime, of saplings, endeavoring to clasp the trunks of trees in their arms, but still going headlong and helplessly on. —William Henry Milburn, *The Pioneers, Preachers and People of the Mississippi Valley.* New York: Derby & Jackson, 1860, 359&360.

Nor was this behavior limited to one setting or branch of the church. Christian Newcomer recorded a meeting of United Brethren where "the power of God was displayed in a most marvelous manner. The whole congregation was moved, and seemed to wave like corn before a mighty wind. Lamentation and mourning was very general. Many were the wounded and slain. Some of the most stubborn sinners fell instantly before the power of God." —Henry G. Spayth, *United Brethren in Christ.* Circleville, OH: Conference Office of the United Brethren in Christ, 1851, 97.

Reuben Yeakel described a congregation's response to the preaching of John Walter:

> The power of God now came upon the congregation, so that sinners literally fell to the ground, as if they had been shot down. Some cried aloud for mercy, others were speechless. ... The labors with penitents continued uninterruptedly until the following morning! Wonderful conversions took place. —R. Yeakel, *Jacob Albright and his Co-Laborers.* Cleveland: Lauer & Yost, 1883, 112&113.

Peter Jones, a Mississauga Methodist preacher in Canada, reported that experiences like these characterized worship among converts near what is now Brantford, Ontario. He said that at one meeting "the overwhelming power of Divine grace descended upon the people, so that the slain of the Lord were seen all over the house. Some praised the Lord aloud, others fell to the floor as if they had been shot, and lay for some time as if dead. One young woman lay in this state about four hours." —Donald B. Smith, *Mississauga Portraits.* Toronto, Buffalo & London: University of Toronto Press, 2013, 54.

Abel Stevens reported similar experiences from the ministry of Nathan Bangs, in which,

> Hearers, hundreds of hearers, would fall as dead men to the earth under a single sermon. The extraordinary scenes called the "jerks" began at one of these meetings. They were rapid, jerking contortions, which seemed to be always the effect, direct or indirect, of religious causes, yet affected not only the religious, but often the most irreligious minds. Violent opposers were suddenly smitten with them. Drunkards, attempting to drown the effect by liquors, could not hold the bottle to their lips; their convulsed arms would drop it, or shiver it against the surrounding trees. Horsemen, charging in upon the meetings to disperse them, were arrested by the strange affection at the very boundaries of the worshiping circles, and were the more violently shaken the more they endeavored to resist the inexplicable power. —Abel Stevens, *The Life and Times of Nathan Bangs, D.D.* New York: Carlton & Porter, 1863, 149&150.

Early western preacher S.R. Beggs describes a revival near Louisville, Kentucky, that "was attended with many extraordinary physical manifestations in which both the converted and the unconverted were alike exercised." One example he gave involved uncontrolled laughter:

> Some laughed so excessively and so long that it seemed as though they would literally "die laughing." Bending backward as far as they could, they would laugh at the top of their voice, then bending forward almost to the ground, they would continue till they well-nigh lost breath, then straightening up and catching breath, they would renew their convulsive

laughter, repeating the same phenomena for an hour or more, till completely exhausted they would fall down in a swoon. The "jerks" were also very common in the prayer meetings.... —S.R. Beggs, *Pages from the Early History of the West and North-West.* Cincinnati: Methodist Book Concern, 1868, 16.

Jacob Young described an incident in his experience:

The circuit preacher exhorted, and a glorious display of Divine power followed. The congregation was melted into tears; I could compare it no nothing but a storm of wind.

As well as I now recollect, the congregation early all rose from their seats, and began to fall upon the floor like trees thrown down by a whirlwind. In a short time nearly all the congregation were upon the floor, some shouting for joy, others crying for mercy. —Jacob Young. *An Itinerant Ohio Pioneer.* Cincinnati: Cranston & Curts; New York: Hunt & Eaton, n.d., 41.

Still another "exercise" was seen in Hopbottom, Pennsylvania, where George Peck tells us, "the Methodists exhibited their joy, in times of the outpouring of the Spirit, in leaping up and down." Hence the name "Hopbottom" or its nickname, "Hoppingbottom." Peck explains:

Hopbottom was famous for the spirituality and zeal of the membership. This was the center of the circuit, and gave tone to the whole. Some of the meetings, to the eye of the outsider, were scenes of confusion. There was much of holy zeal there, but a little mixed up with something like fanaticism. The jumping spirit was often witnessed in the Hopbottom society, and some of the best members, male and female, were occasionally under its influence. When much excited they would commence moving up and down. The movement was perfectly graceful, and yet evidently unstudied. It was one of the phenomena which attended the great religious excitements of early Methodism. —George Peck, *Early Methodism within the Bounds of the Old Genesee Conference.* New York: Carlton & Porter, 1860, 306; 321&322.

To see these "exercises" as merely arcane, insane, or outrageous oddities would be to miss the impact Cartwright saw. He said,

I always looked upon the jerks as a judgment sent from God, first, to bring sinners to repentance; and secondly, to show professors that God could work with or without means, and that he could work over and above means, and do whatsoever seemeth him good, to the glory of his grace and the salvation of the world.

There is no doubt in my mind that, with weak-minded, ignorant, and superstitious persons, there was a great deal of sympathetic feeling with many that claimed to be under the influence of this jerking exercise; and yet, with many, it was perfectly involuntary. It was, on all occasions, my practice to recommend fervent prayer as a remedy, and it almost universally proved an effectual antidote.

Cartwright went on to list other bizarre behaviors "into which the subjects of this revival fell; such as, for instance, as what was called the running, jumping, barking exercise. The Methodist preachers generally preached against this extravagant wildness." Then he listed others that he strongly condemned. Yet somehow he found something of value for that time in these strange occurrences of the jerks. —W.P. Strickland, ed., *Autobiography of Peter Cartwright, The Backwoods Preacher.* New York: Carlton & Porter, 1856, 51.

It may be that no explanation can be satisfactorily given for much of this, except to point to some of the resulting changes in behavior. Jacob Gruber recorded one of these experiences, refusing to explain:

> He thus describes the "jerks," as they were called: "Different classes of persons had them, men and women. Some were happy under this strange excitement, while others were miserable. Their heads would shake in quick motion backward and forward till the person would fall. Some would sit down, others would stand it out though agitated and all in commotion from head to foot. Some of the preachers spoke against these exercises as they did against shouting, and hurt the feelings of sincere persons without doing good to any. ...
>
> Other strange things occurred at his camp-meetings which he describes. The exercises assumed a different aspect at different times and places. Strange and unaccountable as were the jerks, they were, if anything, outdone in the running, jumping, whirling, dancing, pointing, and crying exercises. When he was called upon to explain these things, he replied, "I can't explain what I don't understand. If those who have them cannot understand them how is it possible for me to unravel the mystery. I am not under obligations to analyze or methodize these exercises, having no tools for that work." —W.P Strickland, *The Life of Jacob Gruber.* New York: Carlton & Porter, 1860, 38; 43.

Lorenzo Dow wrote of an experience near Knoxville, Tennessee, where some of the worshippers were seized by the jerks:

> This so excited my attention that I went over the ground to view it; and found where the people had laid hold of them and jerked so powerfully that they had kicked up the earth as a horse stamping flies. I observed some emotion, both this day and night among the people; a Presbyterian minister, with whom I stayed, observed, "Yesterday whilst I was preaching, some had the jerks, and a young man from N. Carolina mimicked

them, out of derision, and soon was seized with them himself, which was the case with many others; ...I observing this, went to him and asked him what he thought of it. Said he, "I believe God sent it on me for my wickedness, and making so light of it in others;" and requested me to pray for him. —Lorenzo Dow, *History of Cosmopolite.* Wheeling: Joshua Martin, 1848, 184.

Charles Giles witnessed many similar phenomena, even when people were away from any revival gathering, praying by themselves or going about other activities. "These occurrences were not only common in the time of public worship, but some were frequently seized while in their secret devotions, at home, and likewise while at their usual employments." He notes that after investigations by ministers and by a medical doctor, no one could explain why certain people were affected and others not, nor could they find medical or other explanations. He also said, "that these operations occur nowhere, under no circumstances, but in religious meetings, or some devout exercise," causing him to conclude that "they must be classed among the marvelous works of the Holy Spirit in the kingdom of grace." The physician concluded, similarly, "that all we could do, in explaining the mystery, was, merely to say, that it is the effect of the power of God, and there leave it. " —Charles Giles, *Pioneer.* New York: G. Lane & P.P. Sandford, 1844, 75-78.

Ezekiel Cooper, one of the earliest preachers in our tradition, addressed this issue, noting that in one revival setting, more than a decade *before* Cane Ridge,

> Many of the most abandoned offenders against God were brought to the experience of true religion. Those who had, a little before, been notorious sinners, could testify of the pardoning love of God in the remission of their sins. This was "the Lord's doing, and it was marvelous in our eyes;" instances of which had great effect in silencing gainsayers. Indeed, what can be more convincing than to look around and see upright, pious men walking circumspectly in the fear of God, who a few month before were enormous perpetrators of the most atrocious crimes?

With this kind of evidence readily at hand, there were those who would turn their criticism toward the bizarre and, to some, repugnant nature of the events themselves:

> Some asked: "Could not those effects be produced without the shouting and noise?" My reply was, generally, I did not know how that might be, but this was certain, they were not produced before, and I doubt that they would have been, had not God worked in this extraordinary manner; for I did not see or hear of any such effects then being so extensive and general except where there was this noise and power attending them. I also

observed it was not the noise that produced the effects, but the effects of the power which produced the noise; though the noise, being principally the effect of God's power among the people, might be attended with a great blessing to the hearers and spectators, as it certainly was. —George A. Phoebus, *Beams of Light on Early Methodism in America.* New York: Phillips & Hunt; Cincinnati: Cranston & Stowe, 1887, 90&91.

Christian Newcomer described "falling" and recovery as indicating God's presence and work in people's lives during a meeting where he was involved. At this gathering, "the Lord was present" and "sinners on every side fell to the floor." Throughout the story he and others tried to explain what was happening:

> Among others was a youth of about thirteen years of age. Some were struck with awe, others flew into a passion, gathered their friends and relatives up, and carried them out of the house, saying this was the work of the devil. I endeavored to persuade them with meekness to let the poor souls alone until their friend should be restored to consciousness; adding, if it is the work of the devil your friends will curse when they revive, and if it is the work of God, they will pray and praise God. They had carried the youth upstairs, and laid him on a bed, watching him with great anxiety. When he recovered from his swoon, he immediately began to praise God. About a dozen of his associates were in distress, confessing that they had sinned against God. They sent down for me to come up and pray for them. Some of them experienced mercy and pardon and they exhorted their friends to fly to the outstretched arms of Sovereign mercy. The meeting continued until after midnight when I had to leave and return to the place where I had preached in the daytime. [Then,] This morning the people assembled again at the house where we lodged. Among them was a man who had behaved rudely at last night's meeting. He cried bitterly and said that he had sinned against God in attributing the work of grace to the devil. He begged humbly for pardon, and besought us to pray for him. Then I exhorted them to prove faithful.... —Samuel S. Hough, ed., *Christian Newcomer.* Dayton: Church of the United Brethren in Christ, 1941, 81&82.

During this episode, the "swoon" experienced by some was variously interpreted as cause to be "struck with awe;" "the work of the devil;" "the work of God," "the work of grace," and cause for "mercy and pardon." Newcomer had patiently worked with the disgruntled people who had experienced "great anxiety," and once the boy revived and praised God, the man who had seen this falling as the devil's work, now believed "he had sinned against God" in saying so.

A very positive assessment of such exercises comes from New England preacher Dan Young. Young and his family were planning to attend a camp meeting when they decided to invite someone to join them. This "young woman ... had been raised in a way which gave her terrible notions about the Methodists, but since she lived with us she had become awakened, and was very desirous of fleeing the wrath to come, and of laying hold of eternal life." She was reluctant to go to the camp meeting, because...

> ...she feared that she would see somebody fall, and that it might have a bad effect on her mind. I told her to go, and mind nothing about what others did, but earnestly pray to God to convert her soul. The meeting soon became interesting and glorious, and this young woman was the first one on the ground who fell, and she remained in deep agony till Jesus spoke to her troubled mind, and she was then unmistakably full of glory and of God, and became a right shouting Methodist. The meeting was one of great power and grace. Many were smitten to the ground, and multitudes were brought to taste that God was gracious, and to witness the power of Christ to forgive sins. Triumphant shouts of the redeemed, and the loud wail of mourners in mingled sounds, made a noise that could be heard afar off. —W.P. Strickland, ed., *Autobiography of Dan Young*. New York: Carlton & Porter, 1860, 171&172. Cf. 261-264.

In his biography of Elijah Hedding, D.W. Clark gave another positive evaluation of such phenomena. Regarding a camp meeting led by Hedding, Clark wrote,

> The people were all amazed and confounded; the scoffer was silenced; the blasphemer turned pale and trembled; the infidel stood aghast. The universal voice was: "Truly this is the mighty power of God; let us adore and tremble before him." That night of glorious power was with multitudes the turning point that thenceforward shaped their destinies heavenward; and in the breasts of hundreds of Christians the holy fire was kindled anew into a more glorious and inextinguishable flame. —D. W. Clark, *Life and Times of Rev. Elijah Hedding, D.D.*. New-York: Carlton & Phillips, 1855, 186.

Reports like these could be multiplied at length, demonstrating that they were not unusual in that early time (though to outsiders, and even many Methodists, they were very strange). Probably the best way to evaluate them is to see them as a work of grace, operating within the worship culture of the revival to reach into the depths of people's souls in order to initiate or deepen the radical transformation of their lives, whether through initial awakening, or conversion, or the forward motion of sanctification. An experience like his would break through the surface of thoughts and emotions. Shallow skepticism or fashionable churchiness would yield to an irresistible encounter with the glory of God and an unforgettable taste of the heavenly kingdom. Perhaps the best Biblical precedent is the example of Peter, James, and John as "they fell to the ground, terrified," at the transfiguration. (Matthew 17:6, NIV) Mark says that Peter's suggestion of building shelters for Jesus, Moses, and Elijah came because "He did not know what to say, they were so frightened." (Mark 9:6, NIV) Luke adds that the experience made them "very sleepy." (Luke 9:32, NIV) But the most important aspect of the entire experience had little to do with falling, fear, or sleepiness – these disciples were, Peter tells us, "eyewitnesses of his majesty." (II Peter 1:16, NIV) Their encounter lifted them up beyond anything they had ever known, and cast them down in understandable astonishment, fear, and awe, for "they saw his glory." (Luke 9:32, NIV)

Whatever the source or meaning of these "exercises," they somehow brought rebellious, violent, sometimes flagrantly sinful, or merely superficial people to their spiritual knees, so that instead of mocking, attacking, socializing, or using these outdoor meetings for their own purposes, they suddenly had to take them seriously, and were perhaps driven to a degree of openness to their transformational purpose. Looking at such things from a great distance of time, culture, and assumptions about worship and Christian behavior, one might well shake one's head and leave it at that. But some who actually witnessed these things could, even if reluctantly, see practical, spiritual benefit – even see them as one of God's teaching methods. Whatever the ultimate determination, they cannot be left out of the story without leaving that story incomplete.

Chapter 15

Application

"But grow in the grace and knowledge of our Lord Jesus Christ. To him be glory both now and forever! Amen." —*II Peter 3:18, NIV*

"The vineyard of the Lord / Before his laborers lies; And lo! we see the vast reward which waits us in the skies." —Charles Wesley, "And Let Our Bodies Part," *The Hymn Book of the Free Methodist Church.* Chicago: Free Methodist Publishing House, 1906, #301, v.3.

This chapter offers a structure and plan for applying the insights and experiences we have explored to churches in the Methodist tradition today and in the future. Clearly there is no point in trying to imitate a bygone era in every detail. Were we to try, we would only end up with a piece of living history suitable for a museum. When we think of obvious ingredients in such a living history, we would need homespun clothing, plenty of horses and equipment, primitive tent camping, and classes in frontier preaching. All of that would be interesting, but beside the point. We would be witnessing only the outer shell of their experience.

Nor do we need to roll back denominational histories to an earlier time, before many of the divisions we live with came to pass. In fact, a focus on institutions, books of Discipline, or the details and legalities of licensing and ordination, would veer well away from any meaningful change. There is no need for all of us to return to a single Bible translation, perhaps comparing it to Wesley's revision, or to limit ourselves to the hymns of any given collection from the past. In fact, the constant blossoming of musical creativity has been a feature of our tradition from the beginning, expressed in Charles Wesley's hymns, constantly revised hymnals, camp meeting and revival song books, and now contemporary Christian music. There are values and deficits in each category, and no single form or collection will serve the entire Wesleyan movement.

The language of our spirituality has also changed. While we must understand the content of that language from our ancestors in order to get at the reality behind it, we are not bound to use each and every word today. On the other hand, the way of salvation must be understood and followed today without getting lost in vague or misleading substitutes. It is hard to imagine replacing expressions like prevenient, justifying, or sanctifying grace. The term "grace" itself is sometimes difficult for people to grasp, but until we come up with a better one, we will have to do the essential work of translation. In the recent past there have been well-intentioned attempts to jettison traditional theological language to accommodate seekers and others for whom that language raises difficulties. Too often the substance has been lost or denatured in the process. A better model might be that of any serious hobby or sport, which has its own language, which each new participant needs to learn and use. The fact that this language is specialized and out of the ordinary, is no argument for its discontinuation. When people actually care about the activity itself, no matter whether it is baseball, gardening, or spiritual growth, they will be motivated to learn and use its terminology.

What is crucial for us today is to understand and practice deeply the heart of what our ancestors called "religion." That term itself has undergone such a sweeping change that it no longer communicates the same reality. The essential reality is what must be revived and lived, even if we need new words to express it. The transformation of each person, made possible by the death and resurrection of Jesus Christ and growing in us by the power of the Spirit, is the essence of what we are all about. That transformation has to be soul deep and not superficial. It must propel us forward on a pathway I have called the road to glory. We must walk that road by grace, all the way through our earthly lives and beyond, because the road shares in and leads to eternal life.

In order for large numbers of Christians in our tradition to see and travel this road, we must help people to see life whole. For too long we have broken people into categories of age, class, ethnicity, and other marks of differentiation. In terms of this study, age is a key factor. As long as people see life in cross section, with each stage in life clearly separated from all the others, they will live in those categories and will not be able to walk a road which connects and transcends them all. We human beings must see each stage of our lives as building on the ones before, and leading to the ones that follow. We need to reflect on the common threads of faith, hope, and love that unite them all and point beyond to their source in God.

Christians especially need to live "the unity of the Spirit through the bond of peace," seeing each other as brothers and sisters in Christ, pilgrims on a journey we all share, using our spiritual gifts to help each other along the road to glory. (Ephesians 4:3, NIV)

In our churches we often seek and program for spiritual growth, but rarely do we ask "to what end?" We want to deepen and improved people's lives, but do we have a vision for what a mature Christian is like? What is the hoped for result of the growth? Where is it heading? It seems that we often value growth for its own sake, without seeing it as preparation for eternity. Thus, seeing life whole pulls us out of generational ruts to see the entire scope of life, so that it is possible to construct ministry for the entire person over time.

One practical application of this principle is expanding the range of our preaching by relating Scripture and its application to issues of life, death, and resurrection; transience vs. eternity, and holiness as the "way to heaven." Even with widespread use of lectionaries, we tend to emphasize those portions of the Bible that address our own "this worldly" concerns; our perceptions of what is needed at the moment. Too often in our time this places the road to glory in a marginal position, if it is included at all. The subject may make an appearance at funerals and memorial services, if we get beyond eulogies and "celebrations of life." All these ingredients are important, but if we fail to address eternity and offer people ultimate hope, we do little more than reflect secular preoccupations. But death and eternity, even if we do a good job of addressing them at funerals, should not be left for those times only. People need to live each day with hope, and hope that is far more than mere optimism.

Optimism may look at each day or period of life with an upbeat attitude that works toward good results or expresses preferences for weather, sports outcomes, or performance on exams. Hope runs deeper than that. Christian hope is a foundational orientation to life that is rooted in our connection with God and our choice of the road to glory. Hope transcends temporary circumstances and focuses on ultimate outcomes. Hope can endure passing disappointments while it looks to the bigger picture of where God is leading. Hope endures where optimism fails. Hope is not a Pollyanna view of reality that downplays evil and death. Instead, hope recognizes evil as a reality that must be dealt with and sees death as our last enemy, which will be decisively overcome. (I Corinthians 15:26) Hope sees the twists and turns of our path as part of a larger pattern of progress toward glory, and looks for glimpses of that glory along the way. Hope should be constantly fed by our experiences of God in worship and in all the means of grace.

Another implication of the circuit riders' approach to death and eternity is their certainty about the truth of Scripture and the basic teachings of orthodox Christianity, as understood and presented in our Wesleyan tradition. It is impossible to seek Scriptural holiness if we no longer see Scripture as true, authoritative, and normative. There is no alternative source of truth and authority that offers solid ground to walk on, or a destiny worth walking toward, if we reject, ignore, or downplay the basic message of the Bible. Everything we know for sure about death and resurrection, heaven and hope, eternity and sanctification, is given to us in Scripture. No church or preacher that ignores, soft pedals, or redefines Scripture can claim continuity with Wesleyan theology, Christian orthodoxy, or the faith of our early Methodist ancestors. No substitute for Scripture can offer us ground for hope. Truth degrades into opinion, which in turn changes with the whims of popular and academic culture.

Preaching that embodies Scripture and our Wesleyan, evangelical tradition looks at life from the vantage point of eternity. Issues are evaluated and priorities chosen on the basis of God's vision for humanity, rather than flawed and quickly passing human agendas. Each milestone in our journey of faith is illuminated by the transfiguring light of Christ, through which we see clearly the meaning of what we experience, and upon which we base our hope.

"For with you is the fountain of life; in your light we see light." (Psalm 36:9, NIV) Light imagery in Scripture tells us a great deal about God as the ever-giving source of light, light expressed and exemplified in Scripture, which is "a light on my path." (Psalm 119:105, NIV) The God who is light, is revealed to us in Jesus, the light of the world. (I John 1:5; John 8:12) Without his light, we "walk in darkness." (John 8:12, NIV) Perhaps the most powerful revelation of that light came to Jesus' disciples, and through them to us, in the Transfiguration, where we read in Matthew, "His face shone like the sun." (Matthew 17:2, NIV) It was at that moment on "the sacred mountain" that the three disciples became "eyewitnesses of his majesty." (II Peter 1:18; 16, NIV) Jesus both shared and promised this light to all who believe and follow him, saying in Matthew, "You are the light of the world," and praying in John, "I want those who have given me to be with me where I am, and to see my glory, the glory you have given me because you loved me before the creation of the world." (Matthew 5:14; John 17:24, NIV)

This light of transfiguration makes the road to glory more than an ordinary journey. It lights our way, provides us with wisdom and knowledge, scatters our darkness and the darkness of our world, and shines at the end of our earthly path to welcome us into God's eternity. This light is spiritual, moral, intellectual, and life-giving. It is this light that people must see in our lives, our worship, and our participation in the world. Any substitute for this light is a distraction coming from the world, beckoning us away from God's road to a place of confusion and misdirection, which we in turn will share with those who need the one light that "shines in the darkness" as "the light of all mankind." (John 1:5; 4, NIV) Substitute "lights" lead us down empty paths, which though popular, lead only "to destruction." (Matthew 7:13, NIV) Such is the "way that appears to be right, but in the end it leads to death." (Proverbs 16:25, NIV) No alternative to the light from God's Word will faithfully express our tradition, or lead people reliably along the road to glory.

The circuit riders and other faithful people of our early tradition lived their lives from the standpoint of eternity. The evaluated competing values by their correspondence (or lack thereof) to the character of God and his vision for humanity. They chose priorities for their lives by their tendency to move them forward on the road to glory. Anything less was a diversion from God's purpose for their lives. Even if that diversion was attractive, popular, respectable, or pleasurable, it must be left by the roadside without regret.

Today our values and priorities are affected by people and things around us, by the standards and distractions of our culture, by social media and media in general, and by compelling appeals to what seems to be our self-interest. Living from the vantage point of eternity gives us a rock to stand on in the constantly shifting sands of this world. It asks us to evaluate every option and every action by where it leads. Will it fulfill or distract us from our God-given purpose in life? Is it consistent with what we know about God? Does it flow from love or selfishness? Will it lead to heaven or hell? Without an eternal vision, life becomes a chaotic contest of momentary impulses and culturally generated values. Instead of being "rooted and established in love," meaning "the love of Christ," we are easily "tossed back and forth by the waves, and blown here and there by every wind of teaching and by the cunning and craftiness of people in their deceitful scheming." (Ephesians 3:17&18; 4:14, NIV) This is hard enough and destructive enough when we are "out there in the world;" it is devastating when it happens in our churches.

To understand life and its meaning, to choose among attractive options, and to see where the road we are taking actually leads, all of us require a place to stand. An old gospel hymn puts this in the context of hope, saying, "My hope is built on nothing less than Jesus' blood and righteousness. I dare not trust the sweetest frame, but wholly lean on Jesus' name." The hymn goes on to affirm trust "in his unchanging grace" in the midst of temporary darkness, for even "When all around my soul gives way, he then is all my hope and stay." The last verse visualizes the worshipper, after a life of conversion and sanctification, standing "faultless ... before the throne." This eternal, hope-filled perspective allows us to say, in joyful, thankful praise, "On Christ the solid rock I stand, all other ground is sinking sand; all other ground is sinking sand." —Edward Mote, "My Hope Is Built," *The United Methodist Hymnal.* Nashville: The United Methodist Publishing House, 1989, #368.

When we stand on the "solid rock," informed by Scripture and living in the light of eternity, we are able to discover and enjoy the life God has for us, instead of wasting our lives in a meandering succession of "trivial pursuits." God's perspective is available to us as we sort through the clamor of life's demands, attractions, distractions, and alternative directions. We can live with confidence, though always in the knowledge that we must be open to reliable counsel and correction. We have access to the source of all genuine inspiration and all the resources of grace to live victoriously, even when we cannot avoid setbacks and sorrows. We find in the vision of Christian perfection the highest possible standard and goal in life, and we are offered the power to reach it.

Hope is at work and growing when we are committed to continual spiritual growth, in every age and circumstance of our lives. There is joy in growing deeper and stronger in God's love; growing in knowledge and application of things that matter, and drawing closer and closer to God in prayer and worship. There is surpassing, all-encompassing joy in knowing where we are going; knowing that God is with us throughout our journey, and knowing that our trajectory leads to the very best future imaginable.

There is great peace in being able, as many of our early preachers did, to stand back from our busyness and take stock of where our road has taken us, and where it is going. To break free from hectic schedules and responsibilities to look backward and forward in the Spirit is to value where God has brought us, and what blessings he has for us down the road. That kind of reflective remembering deepens our souls and connects us more completely with the God of our past and our destiny.

One great insight that can help us as we travel through life, is to realize that each stage in our lives is rich in God's blessings. Knowing this is a blessing in itself, and prepares us for whatever may be ahead. So often we look back with regret or nostalgia, or forward in fear or unrealistic optimism. But cutting through all that is the sure awareness that God has been there all along, and he will never leave us. Psalm 71 prays, "Do not cast me away when I am old; do not forsake me when my strength is gone." And then, "Even when I am old and gray, do not forsake me, my God...."

(Psalm 71: 9&18, NIV) This is a very natural plea, especially in a society that values, even worships youth and all too often turns its back on old age. No doubt a major reason for society forsaking older people is its lack of hope for anything beyond. Childhood and youth are filled with hope and forward movement, like an exciting adventure, with one new and rewarding episode after another. Old age is, in one respect, a time for letting go, for giving up on once treasured pursuits. Actually, the limitations of aging are nothing in light of eternity, but a society that has lost sight of eternity, by definition, cannot see the hope that eternity holds.

Along with the pleas for God not to forsake us, the Psalms contain other perspectives on age. One sees the reality that, for some, old age is a time for renewed vitality and meaningful engagement. Thus we read in Psalm 92, "The righteous will flourish like a palm tree, they will flourish like a cedar of Lebanon; planted in the house of the Lord, they will flourish in the courts of our God. They will still bear fruit in old age, they will stay fresh and green...." (Psalm 92:12-14, NIV) This Psalm offers hope for productive older years, connected to one's life "in the courts of God." Still another perspective on aging is found in Psalm 37, where David realizes, "I was young and now I am old, yet I have never seen the righteous forsaken...." (Psalm 37:25, NIV) The memory of past blessing offers encouragement to hope for whatever may come next.

When people are actively engaged in Christian life and work, making the contribution their gifts empower them to make, connected to God in worship and Christian fellowship, they can flourish and continue growing indefinitely. Such people can be found in most of our churches. The hope expressed in this Psalm is amplified and extended tremendously, however, when seen in the context of *eternal* life. Because of the glory of eternity, there never needs to be an end to growth or to hope.

Too many opportunities for this kind of reflection and flourishing are taken away when we segregate people in our churches by age and stage in life. Not only does each stage have its blessings, but we become more aware of those blessings by living our Christian lives together. Much has been said and done in recent years about strategic targeting of particular groups in society, programming for "affinity groups," and capitalizing on the shared experiences of people going through a given stage in life. We see this reflected in churches that have focused on a very limited target audience, and in churches that divide people for most of their programs. There may be some communities where a local congregation will naturally attract young families or retirees, but in many others there can be a richness of diversity that encourages people to share their experience with those younger and older than themselves. In such churches, the blessings that attend each stage in life are there for all to see, and not only to remember or imagine. When intergenerational connections become normal and strong, communication across those lines becomes natural and free. Each person, regardless of age or experience, is able to "flourish in the courts of our God." In a similar way, wherever possible, churches are richer and healthier when they include people from a variety of occupations and social classes; educational experiences and ethnic backgrounds.

When eternity is the shared goal of every member of a congregation, they all benefit from recognizing each other as fellow pilgrims on the road to a glory they all hope and even expect to enjoy. They appreciate a much wider range of Christian experience, learning from each other what only the others can teach. Christian education, on Sundays in church or at any time or place, equips people for this journey. The topics covered in Sunday schools and other formats should always include the life of spiritual growth leading to, and participating in, eternity. People should never reach old age unprepared to see themselves and their time in life from God's perspective, with the grace, hope, and continuing preparation appropriate to their stage in life. How can a faith that is so rich in the resources of grace, Scripture, Christian biography, and educational materials leave these most important matters untaught?

While there are practical reasons to specialize in age or interest-based classes, there are also good reasons to bring people together at times and to see each other as fellow learners on a common path. One of the older ways churches did this was by having an opening and/or closing "exercise" in which all took part, before or after dispersing to age-determined classes. Even if that is not workable or desirable today, there are other venues for bringing people together – in fellowship meals, mission projects, class meetings, and most of all in worship. I knew of one church where students came to confirmation class having never attended Sunday worship, because for all those years they were segregated into nursery and junior church.

What a terrible loss to them, and to their congregation! How were they expected to make a commitment to a church that had kept them isolated, whose worship they had never shared?

Many churches will have older people who exemplify the Christian journey, whose lives offer encouragement to younger and middle aged Christians and whose perspectives on faith and life should be honored and treasured. We should be looking to them much as an earlier generation looked to people's death bed scenes, to gain wisdom and strength for an experience not yet our own, so that when we get there, we will have waymarks to go by. A congregation that lacks older people will have to look elsewhere for this kind of modeling. One useful way to connect youth with people older than themselves (though not necessarily *very* old), is to invite members of confirmation classes (or their equivalent) to choose exemplary adults as mentors. In my experience, young people have shown great wisdom in the people they choose, and when the youth and their mentors follow through with personal conversations and encouragement, the experience becomes a rich exercise – for both – in building stronger disciples.

Preachers today, as in circuit rider days, must recruit and equip the people of our churches for the way of salvation, emphasizing heaven itself and the road that leads there. Grace-filled preaching will turn away from legalistic, moralistic sermons that demand changes in behavior without offering the grace needed to empower those changes. Preaching in the light of eternity will turn from a cafeteria of unrelated topics to an approach that relates all topics to life in grace and the road to glory. Preachers should picture themselves as travel guides, eager to walk the road and to convince others to join them. They must see that all passengers on the train that is "bound for glory," are fed the spiritual food they need for their next steps. They must coordinate the gifts of the Spirit within each congregation, and even in the larger fellowship of churches, to see that everyone has the equipment needed to "grow in the grace and knowledge of our Lord and Savior Jesus Christ." (II Peter 3:18, NIV). To do this, they will have to work primarily from the abundant spiritual resources of God's grace, rather than principles adapted from the world. Preachers themselves will need God's "grace and peace … in abundance," enough for their own walk and that of those they lead. (II Peter 1:2, NIV)

One of the chief endeavors of preachers during the circuit rider era was evangelism. The term "evangelical" has been confused and devalued considerably in recent years, but in those days its meaning was very clear. Christians, especially those who stood in pulpits and prayed at revival "altars," did all they could to bring non-believers or superficial believers into a deep, lifelong relationship with Christ. They did it primarily through persuasion, through word and example, by helping people to see, hear, and feel the glorious reality of God and the terrible prognosis that came with continuing to live without God. They contrasted the wide and narrow roads, the beauty of heaven and the pain of hell, the destructiveness of sin and the boundless hope of glory. They did it through Scripture, song, story, and example; in personal conversation and public worship.

Conversion meant decisively turning away from sin and self-centeredness and turning to God's love and holiness. It began with conviction of, or awakening to, one's own sinfulness, including a clear awareness of the seriousness and wages of sin. It moved through a time of mourning and

144   Circuit Riders on the Road to Glory

anguish as people realized where they stood before God, crying out for mercy and a new life. Mourning was followed by a clear sense of God's forgiveness and a powerful experience of his presence, and of the sacramental nature of all around them. The new convert was bathed in grace and, at least for a moment, saw life, creation, and other people as God saw them, and as they were meant to be. That experience launched them into disciplined discipleship through the means of grace, including those extraordinary means they found in class meetings and further revival. The twin goals for that discipleship were transformation by the power of the Spirit, and final transition into the heavenly kingdom. In the meantime, converted Christians turned around and sought to be God's instruments in converting and discipling others.

In those early days, the churches in our Methodist family were "good at" doing evangelism. They were evangelical by nature. Growth in numbers demonstrated that. They were also good at accessing the power of the Spirit for good works, from reform movements to building churches and colleges, to sending missionaries and influencing the whole tenor of society. There was no radical separation between faith and works. Activist faith defined what evangelicalism was all about.

Somehow, the movement that once set about "reform[ing] the continent, and spread[ing] Scripture-holiness over these lands" lost much of its instinct, enthusiasm, and even ability to carry out that mission. Some branches of our movement maintained their commitment and practice of evangelism longer than others, and some continue with a vigor they never lost, or have somehow regained. Some members of Methodist denominations question whether evangelism matters at all, or wonder what place it still holds in an age of religious diversity. No doubt many who read the stories of old time camp meetings find them bizarre, incomprehensible, and perhaps even repugnant in light of contemporary assumptions and norms. Many are embarrassed by examples of badly done evangelism, or evangelists who disgrace the name, and would rather move on to other forms of church activity. For many, Christian education has replaced evangelism as the primary means of recruiting and training new disciples. Many in our churches are not "good at" evangelism, and resist any involvement in it. Many others are so distracted by other issues and concerns they might not even give evangelism a thought. —*The Doctrines and Discipline of the Methodist Episcopal Church.* Philadelphia: Henry Tuckness, 1797, iii.

But evangelism is not only essential to our Wesleyan identity; it is essential to the gospel itself. Walking away from evangelism (or another name, if you prefer, for the same activity) means walking away from the One who said:

"All authority in heaven and on earth has been given to me. Therefore go and make disciples of all nations, baptizing them in the name of the Father and of the Son and of the Holy Spirit, and teaching them to obey everything I have commanded you. And surely I am with you always, to the very end of the age." (Matthew 28:18-20, NIV)

"But you will receive power when the Holy Spirit comes on you; and you will be my witnesses in Jerusalem, and in all Judea and Samaria, and to the ends of the earth." (Acts 1:8, NIV)

To resist, refuse, downplay, or redefine evangelism is to turn our churches away from all that we know of earliest Christianity and its apostolic leaders; to trivialize what we mean by "church" and to leave its mission behind. What can a lethargic, declining, self-absorbed, or culturally conformed church do with descriptions like these from the Book of Acts?

Those who accepted his [Peter's] message were baptized, and about three thousand were added to their number that day. (Acts 2:41, NIV)

And the Lord added to their number daily those who were being saved. (Acts 2:47, NIV)

Day after day, in the temple courts and from house to house, they never stopped teaching and proclaiming the good news that Jesus is the Messiah. (Acts 5:42, NIV)

So the word of God spread. The number of disciples in Jerusalem increased rapidly, and a large number of priests became obedient to the faith. (Acts 6:7, NIV)

Then the church throughout Judea, Galilee and Samaria enjoyed a time of peace and was strengthened. Living in the fear of the Lord and encouraged by the Holy Spirit, it increased in numbers. (Acts 9:31, NIV)

...and a great number of people were brought to the Lord. (Acts 11:24, NIV)

But the word of God continued to spread and flourish. (Acts 12:24, NIV)

A decision by a church in our Methodist tradition, even if it is made subconsciously, gradually, or unintentionally, to move away from Jesus' commission, from the example of the early Church, and from the primary purpose found in the New Testament letters, has left much more than its Methodist identity behind.

So we may need a new word for evangelism. We may find that some of the old methods for doing evangelism need considerable revision or change. Our preaching may need to change to meet the requirements of clear and compelling communication in today's world. But we are unfaithful to the gospel and the living tradition of Methodism and Christianity itself, if we say that evangelism no longer matters; that spreading the good news is outdated and unrealistic, or that the spiritual encounter between each person and the Lord of heaven and earth is an optional experience, of no particular consequence for time or eternity.

It is no good for a person or church to claim Methodist identity while substituting a completely different purpose as its reason for existence. Nor is it good enough to pay lip service to evangelism and do nothing about it. If we have learned anything from the lives and reflections of early Methodist preachers, it is that *everything* depends on one's participation in the road to glory, beginning with the decision to take that road in the first place. If their experience is a reliable indication, we will also find that a church that places evangelism and growth in discipleship as its first outreach priority, will also find that its social witness will be stronger than if social witness were given first place. We will also find that our social witness will be an expression of God's grace and truth, justice and peace in the world, rather than a baptized version of someone's social or political agenda. For essential, original Methodism, every position taken on a moral or social issue had to pass muster first with the word and character of God. So it should be with us.

Among the themes we have discovered in the writings by and about circuit riders and other Methodist preachers, is the prominence of revival as a primary expression of evangelism and spiritual growth. It will seem to many that, in spite of the importance and obvious success of revival in our early days, times have changed and revival will have to change if it is to have a future. Already evangelists and others have tried media as the delivery system for revival. Yet the immediate reaction of many to the term "TV evangelist" points to the problem with that platform. Christian messages abound on the internet, and particularly on social media. It would seem at this point that these contribute to Christian education and discipleship in various ways, but they do not seem to be equivalents for revival itself. Some local churches may continue services that resemble old-time revivals, and we can hope these will have good results. Christian conferences and music festivals resemble portions of the revival experience, but their impact as instruments of evangelism seems limited, and sometimes tied to the entertainment that comes as part of the presentation. The kind of widespread, culture-wide revivals that swept across North America and beyond do not yet seem to have made their appearance. When they do, and as they do, we need to be ready. Until they do, we need unceasing prayer. We need to be on the lookout for the kind of revival that will flourish in a post-revival church and world. There is no substitute for recruiting and equipping people for the road to glory.

Class meetings played a vital part in conserving the fruit of revival in the early days, though they were already beginning to fade by the mid-nineteenth century. However, this generation is seeing a rediscovery and adaptation of the class meeting that can accomplish similar results. Prominent in these efforts is the work of Kevin Watson, whose books on class and (with Scott Kisker) band meetings are being used as handbooks for churches wanting to start this kind of ministry. They are at the center of the New Room movement centered at Asbury Theological Seminary, and a version of the class meeting is operational in the "reunion groups" of the Upper Room's Walk to Emmaus. In many places there are small accountability groups that may be unaware of traditional class meetings, even as they accomplish a similar purpose. While evangelism and spiritual growth on the road to glory are essential to Christianity and our own Methodist identity, class meeting remain useful instruments. Colorado circuit rider John Lewis Dyer wrote, "I have always believed the class-meeting to be one of the greatest means of grace in the spiritual economy of the Church." —Kevin Watson, *The Class Meeting, (etc.)*. Wilmore KY: Seedbed, 2014; Kevin Watson & Scott Kisker, *The Band Meeting, (etc.)*. Franklin, TN: Seedbed, 2017. John Lewis Dyer, *The Snow-Shoe Itinerant*. Cincinnati: Cranston & Stowe, 1890, 25.

Dyer's testimony to the importance of class meetings was echoed throughout the movement. These small gatherings brought fellowship and encouragement to people who would otherwise be isolated in their faith and possibly lost between the mountain top experiences that came with camp and quarterly meetings. They allowed for disciple making and conscientious supervision by class leaders and pastors. In some of today's class meetings, people may hesitate to take on that supervisory role, but when they do, they will find it helpful to their own pilgrimage, even as they may save others from falling away or growing lax.

Just as class meetings empowered small groups within the churches, camp and quarterly meetings gathered larger groups from across whole regions. While these functioned as engines for evangelism, they also provided a larger fellowship within which to find inspiration and encouragement. Especially helpful were times of singing, love-feasts, extended prayer, and Holy Communion. These means of grace, packaged together over several days, were reliable conduits for the Holy Spirit to work in the lives of people and their churches. The fellowship among preachers was by itself a great blessing, but that fellowship extended to the whole gathered community. Just as the class meeting needs to be adapted and implemented widely in today's churches, so do regional, and now state, national, and even international gatherings of our people. Such gatherings have sometimes been employed by denominations, though not always with a purpose that is theologically orthodox or spiritually helpful. But there are many examples of large gatherings of Methodist, evangelical, or ecumenical organizations that help people gain perspective and carry out important mission work. In Egypt, for examples, there have been gigantic "youth conferences" that have brought young adults together for worship, teaching, and prayer in the midst of an often dangerous environment.

Historically, the Epworth League and summer church camps provided regional learning and fellowship for smaller numbers. Camps and Bible conferences still serve that function. There seems to be a need for worship and Christian connectedness in ever-widening circles, from two or three friends who find Christ present in their midst (Matthew 18:20), to class meetings of a dozen or so, to congregations of any size, to regional gatherings that might be in the hundreds, to even larger events that could include thousands. Whether they are called by traditional Methodist names is less important than whether they accomplish a similar purpose. No congregation is sufficient unto itself. Its members need both smaller and larger fellowships for very different purposes.

Churches and their participants also need to raise the bar considerably on their level of commitment. In a world that screams for our attention day and night, that organizes a myriad of activities that compete with those of the churches, and that asks us to downgrade the Church to a lower priority than those activities, we will need to recover the centrality of our faith and its expression in churches. People made great sacrifices to attend worship at a time when travel was difficult and transportation could be rough. They set aside blocks of several days at a time, several times each year, to attend quarterly and camp meetings. They lived by the beliefs and values of Christianity even under persecution, as many of our brothers and sisters do in countries around the world today. We need to restore our faith and its communal expression to its rightful place. Casual participation when we feel like it is an affront to God and to our own purpose as God's people. When people from churches living under persecution see the haphazard, shallow commitment of many in North America, they are rightly concerned and may question our sincerity. One expression from our tradition describes true Methodists as earnest Christians, people who take their faith seriously, who try their level best to live in a way that is consistent with their stated beliefs and values. This is the kind of radical commitment Jesus and his apostles called for in New Testament times, and we are fooling ourselves if we think God has lowered his standards to suit us.

As we have seen over and over again, worship offered opportunities for people to see and enter the kingdom of God from time to time, as they walked the road to glory. Worship was neither routine, nor perfunctory. From a tiny congregation where the preacher "talked just like heaven and earth were coming together;" to a class meeting where "Floods of glory and light, from heaven, came pouring in upon us from the upper world;" to camp meetings that were "the borderland of heaven," worship was their window, through which they could glimpse their own longed for, eternal future. —John Berry McFerrin, *Methodism in Tennessee, 1818-1840*. Nashville: Southern Methodist Publishing House, 1873, III: 49; James P. Horton, *A Narrative of the Early Life, Remarkable Conversion, and Spiritual Labors of James P. Horton*. n.c.: Printed for the Author, 1839, 203; Andrew Carroll, in Russell E. Richey, *Methodism in the American Forest*. Oxford & New York: Oxford University Press, 2015, 131.

From this "heaven below" they could see far along the road to glory and find strength, healing, and encouragement to continue traveling that road. This was their "hope, the perspective by which we look into another and better world." This would be the culmination of their travels on the road of sanctifying grace, for "Our destiny is to become what he created us to be, and that destiny unfolds in eternity." —Lorenzo Dow, *History of Cosmopolite*. Wheeling: Joshua Martin, 1848, 491; D. Gregory Van Dussen, *Circuit Rider Devotions*. Lexington: Emeth Press, 2019, 675.

While there is no point in trying to re-create the exact *form* of worship of bygone days, there is every reason to reclaim its *purpose*. Old-time Methodist worship sought to bring about a living connection between God and his people and to open the flood gates of heaven for the outpouring of his Spirit. No matter what size the gatherings might be, they shared this purpose in common. They brought heaven and earth together in such a way as to give people clearer vision of their destination, and grace for the journey to that destination.

While stories, songs, and powerful rhetoric were part of the mix of this worship, they were not there to entertain or to provide a forum for sharing the preachers' opinions. Their purpose was to put people in touch with the living, transforming God, who saved and sanctified them by his presence and power. People attending such worship were certainly entertained by eloquence, music, humor, or a powerful, even melodious voice, but entertainment was not the point. Gatherings like quarterly and camp meetings affirmed their group identity, yet important as this was, it remained secondary to their main concern. Worship became "heaven below," which gave them access to heaven above. Fellowship was unity in Christ and not merely human friendship, though both were happening. Instead, Wesleyan worshippers found that through worship they came to "participate in the divine nature, having escaped the corruption in the world caused by evil desires." (II Peter 1:4, NIV) Worship was part of their transformation, and also prepared them for further transformation down the road.

Worship meant leaving the world behind and entering God's kingdom through opening the gates of heaven. While the shape of Methodist worship facilitated this experience, this purpose does not require a particular style of worship. For example, Orthodox Christians, whose worship is highly structured, deeply sacramental, and richly symbolic, have long seen entering their churches as moving into God's kingdom. The sanctuary, filled with icons of Christ and the saints, provides access to another world, a world that is continuous with the longed-for destination of worshippers. Symbolically and spiritually, the worship space participates in heaven, just as those who enter that space are empowered to participate in the very nature of God, without losing the creature/creator distinction. The worship cultures of Orthodox and early Wesleyan churches could scarcely by father apart, but the essence and purpose of their worship have a surprising correspondence.

Worship for early Methodists – and many other Christians, though they differ in form and culture – meant receiving glimpses of heaven, which in turn empowered their journey toward heaven. It is this essential nature of worship that we must recover in our churches today. God must take the initiative in making this happen. Our relationship with him is not like a vending machine, where we can make him fit into our lives by manipulating his involvement, following well-established precedents. However, elements of those precedents, which have come to us from every age of the Church, including that of early Methodism, often prove resilient and transferable to new situations. Whether the components and style of worship are creative and new, or tried and true, the primary issue cannot be form, but substance. Worship should facilitate a transformative encounter with God. Those who plan and lead worship must ask how we can make ourselves open and available for God to act in our hearts and congregations during worship. How can we create an atmosphere in which God reaches deeply into our hearts, enables us to change direction, and launches us into deeper and stronger discipleship? How can we get beyond *conventions* of worship to the *power* of worship? How will heaven open for us, so that the Spirit fills and surrounds us with life-giving love, wisdom, and strength? Without copying the shape of early Methodist worship, we cannot stop short of its purpose, which was to provide a connection between heaven and earth; God and his people, and in that experience to grow in grace along the road to glory. Nothing short of this is genuine Methodist worship.

The experiences participants relate to us in Methodist literature go far beyond what most of us have known in our own worship, again, not so much in form as in what is accomplished. How do we approach worship with the expectation that God will be there for us and in us to the depth our ancestors knew? The Northumbria Community has as the basis for their life together the twin principles of vulnerability and availability. Could these be at least part of the way to realize the full potential of worship, including fellowship, for our time? —*Northumbria Community, Celtic Daily Prayer.* London, UK: HarperCollins, 2005, 9.

The richness of our Methodist and Christian heritage is such that worship and church life can exist in a variety of forms within an even larger variety of cultures. Surely the fact that worship has brought worshippers into God's presence; has been a place where heaven and earth come together, and has been the primary engine of Christian life, tells us something about its capacity to do the same now and in the future. The key will be to mine that richness for ingredients that bring us closer to God, but even more, to seek the One who has reached out to us when we could only seek him and cry out for salvation.

Methodists today and tomorrow, must cast aside limiting notions of what God can and will do in our lives, especially through worship. We need to appreciate the legacy that comes to us through our ancestors in faith, and embrace the future with eager and open hearts. In the early days of our movement, some of the older, superannuated [retired] preachers complained a good deal that the churches and preachers of the present were not measuring up to their experiences in the past. These "croakers" ["One that croaks, murmurs, of grumbles; one who complains unreasonably." Croaking was "The act of foreboding evil...."] lamented the passing of that earlier time, and wondered whether the future offered enough hope. —*Noah Webster, An American Dictionary of the English Language.* Springfield, MA: George & Charles Merriam, 1848, 285.

One preacher who did some croaking as he looked back over his career, finally came to a better and wiser place. Marmaduke Pearce, after a long ministry, wrote these words to historian George Peck: "Here I am decrepit, crabbed, praising old things, and old times, and old preachers, and scolding the preened preachers, and all they do, and what they don't do, but all to no purpose; so I have pretty nearly given it up, perhaps the sooner the better." To fulfill this resolve, Pearce concluded, "Let us, dear brother, thank God for all that is past, troubles and all, and trust him for all that is to come." —George Peck, *Early Methodism within the Bounds of the Old Genesee Conference.* New York: Carlton & Porter, 1860, 344.

Pearce's words show great and useful wisdom as we look back to the days of circuit riders on the road to glory, and as we muster hope for the unknown days ahead. For in seeking hope and eternal life, we depend not so much on the people or customs of any given era, but on the God "who is, and who was, and who is to come, the Almighty." (Revelation 1:8, NIV) He is both "our help in ages past" and "our hope for years to come." "For in him we live and move and have our being." We have found the hand of God very much at work in our past. Now we turn our eyes toward heaven, ready to serve that same God in the work he is now, and will be doing, on the road to glory. —Revelation 1:8, NIV; Isaac Watts, "O God! our Help in Ages Past," *The Hymnary of the United Church of Canada.* Toronto: United Church Publishing House, 1930, 107, v. 1; Acts 17:28, NIV.

www.ingramcontent.com/pod-product-compliance
Lightning Source LLC
Chambersburg PA
CBHW071429160426
43195CB00013B/1850